CXC EXCEL SERIES

MICROSOFT WORD 2000

& Windows

Delize Williams
Delroy Williams

CRITIQUE

This book is informative, easy to read and its inclusion of various graphics makes it user friendly. The chapters in the text meet the required wordprocessing objectives set by CXC. The practical exercises provide excellent practice for the students. This book is a must for the teachers of Information Technology and all students who will be sitting Information Technology in CXC. I will also recommend this text to anyone who would like to do a beginner's course in word processing.

Paul Stewart (B. Sc., Information Technology)
Teacher, Information Technology
Belair High School
Jamaica.

This book is an ideal resource for the person(s) desirous of learning Microsoft Word. It is thorough, easy-to-understand and relevant. An excellent choice for an introductory to intermediate course in Microsoft Word that also serves as a valuable reference for the Microsoft Word professional.

Jonah Chisholm (B. Sc., Computer and Electrical Engineering)
Assistant Manager, Computer Engineering
Fiscal Services Ltd.
Jamaica.

The book conveys information in a very detailed step-by-step manner and as such it facilitates easy comprehension. As a teacher who has and continues to prepare students for the Information Technology CXC Examination, I strongly recommend this book to CXC students. It expertly covers the necessary topics and provides good resource material.

Charmaine Cousins (B. Sc., Computer Science and Management)
Teacher, Information Technology, Jamaica College

First Edition, 2001
10 9 8 7 6 5 4 3 2 1

Illustrations and images: Reproduced with permission from Microsoft Corporation.

Editorial & Production: Julia Tan (Singapore)

Cover Design: Julia-Mei Tan/Delize & Delroy Williams

Typeset in TNR

Typesetting by: Michelle M.A. Mitchell (Jamaica)

Published by: LMH Publishing Limited
7 Norman Road,
LOJ Industrial Complex
Building 10
Kingston C.S.O., Jamaica
Tel: 876-938-0005; 938-0712
Fax: 876-928-8038
Email: lmhpublishing@cwjamaica.com

Printed and bound by Lightning Source Inc., USA   ISBN 976-610-288-0

PREFACE

This **CXC Excel Series** has been prepared to develop the student's skills in the various subjects of the CXC Examination.

Each book is written by specialists in accordance to the latest curriculum requirements. Text and practice papers are both comprehensive and varied providing the student with ample exposure to the type of questions usually encountered in the examination. The approach is methodical, enabling the student to systematically assimilate the subject matter.

Every book in this series is so specifically geared to the CXC Examination that it truly becomes a tool enhancing the chances for success in this all important Caribbean Examination.

CONTENTS

CHAPTER 1

INTRODUCING WINDOWS

At the end of this chapter you should be able to:-
- Perform the three mouse actions.
- Start a programme.
- Close a window.
- Label the different parts of a window.
- Minimize a window.
- Maximize and restore a window.
- Move and change the size of a window.
- Explain the significance of some of the features observed on a menu.
- Create, copy, move and rename directories and sub-directories.

Learning how to use computers is fun and easier than most people think. As long as you have a positive attitude and an eagerness to learn, you will be fine.

STARTING WINDOWS

When you turn on your computer you are starting Windows. On starting Windows, you will see the taskbar and icons. These comprise the desktop.

THE TASKBAR

    Start

The taskbar is located at the bottom of the screen. It contains the **Start button**. With the Start button you can perform almost any task, such as starting programmes, opening documents and much more.

FOOTNOTE
*Programmes/programs are used synonymously in the book. The British spelling is preferred for the text proper. When the Americanized spelling **program** appears, it refers to the actual Microsoft program application and usage.*

ICONS

Small on-screen pictures are called *icons*. On your screen you should see icons with labels such as *My Computer* and *Recycle Bin*. Each icon represents an object, such as programme. Icons can be used to start programmes.

At this point you need to take a closer look at the mouse. (Do not panic, it is not an animal!)

USING THE MOUSE

In Windows the mouse is usually used. You should observe that as you move the mouse, an arrow moves on the screen. This is your *pointer*. When using the mouse, position the pointer *exactly over* the object you want to select, then press the left mouse button.

The following table describes the various *click actions* that can be performed using the mouse.

ACTION	PURPOSE	PROCEDURE
Clicking	Used to select something.	Briefly press the left button.
Double Clicking	Used to start programmes.	Press the left button twice, quickly.
Dragging	Used to highlight areas on the screen or to move objects around the screen.	Keep the left mouse button depressed while you slide the mouse in the desired direction. Then, release it.
Right-clicking	Used to produce a shortcut menu display.	Briefly press the right mouse button once.

You will be using terminologies very often [i.e. click, double-click, drag]. So if you forget what each means, just quickly refer to the above table to jolt your memory.

STARTING A PROGRAMME

Windows will introduce you to programmes such as *Calculator, WordPad* and *Paint*. Let us start one of these programmes now. *WordPad* is easy enough for any beginner.

To start a programme in Windows:-

1. Click on the *Start* button. (Lightly press the left button on the mouse.)

2. Move the pointer up to the word *Programs*. (A *secondary menu* appears on the right.) (Notice that a blue bar encloses the word *Programs*.)

3. Slide the mouse to the right, along the blue bar that encloses the word *Programs* until your pointer appears in the secondary menu.

   (This can be very tricky. If you make an error, you have to start again from step #1. But do not worry; this just takes practice.)

4. Move your pointer to the word *Accessories*. (The blue bar appears again and so does another secondary menu.)

5. Slide the mouse to the right along the blue bar that encloses the word *Accessories*, until your pointer appears in the secondary menu.

6. Now move your pointer down to the *WordPad* and click.

7. The window for the *WordPad* programme appears. **CONGRATULATIONS!** You have just started the *WordPad* programme.

NOTE

In Windows, all information is displayed in on-screen boxes or *windows*. When a programme is started, a window opens.
(You can also start a programme by double-clicking on the programme's icon.)

CLOSING A WINDOW

When a window is closed, the respective programme is no longer running. Thus you have actually exited this programme.

✓ To close a window, simply click on the window's *Close button* at the top right hand corner of the window...

Close the *WordPad* window and try to start the programme again.

Now, you can actually open some of the interesting programmes such as *Calculator* and *Paint*. To access these, you must first click on *Start*. Then click on *Programs*. Next click on *Accessories*. Upon reaching *Accessories*, look carefully for *Calculator* in the secondary menu, and click on it.

THE PARTS OF A WINDOW

A *window* is made up of *buttons* and *bars* that allow us to manipulate the window.

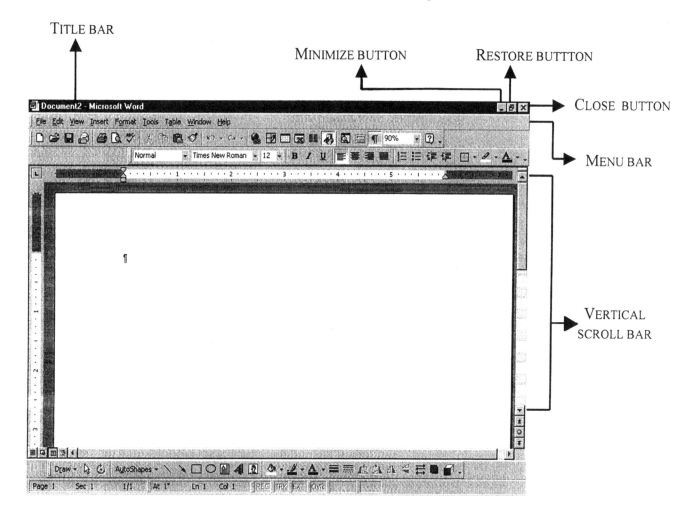

TITLE BAR

MINIMIZE BUTTON

RESTORE BUTTTON

CLOSE BUTTON

MENU BAR

VERTICAL SCROLL BAR

USING THE SCROLL BARS

The presence of *scroll bars* usually indicates that there is more information to view than that which presently appears in the window. There are two types of scroll bars: the *vertical scroll bar* and the *horizontal scroll bar*. Scroll bars allow you to move 'hidden' information into view.

✓ On the vertical scroll bar:-

1. Click on the button with an upward arrow to scroll up.
2. Click on the button with downward arrow to scroll down.

   (Use the horizontal scroll bar if desirous of scrolling to the left or right.)

Within the scroll bar is a little box that moves as you click on the arrows on the bar. This is the *scroll box*. When the box ceases to move, this is an indication that there is no more text to view in that particular direction.

Now you will learn how to perform the following actions:-

- Minimize a window.
- Maximize a window.
- Restore a window.
- Move a window.
- Resize a window.

MINIMIZING A WINDOW

When you minimize a window , you move it out of view temporarily, but it is still active. (The programme is still running). It is similar to playing a videocassette in the VCR while the television is off. Although you do not see the movie on the television screen, the VCR is still in operation.

When a programme's window is minimized, it disappears, but a button appears on the taskbar with the name of the programme.

✓   To minimize a window, click on the *Minimizing button.*

(If you wish to open the window again, simply click on the window's button on the taskbar.)

TRY IT:

1. Start the *WordPad* programme again.

2. Minimize it by clicking on the *Minimize button*.

3. Reopen the window again by clicking on the programme's button on the *Task bar*.

NOTE

Remember, whenever you see a programme's button on the taskbar, it means that the programme is open/running.

MAXIMIZING AND RESTORING A WINDOW

When a window is maximized, it is increased to its largest size.

To maximize a window simply click on the *Maximize button*.

When a window has been maximized, the *Maximize button* disappears, and the *Restore button* appears in its place. This button, when clicked, will restore the window to its original size.

TRY IT:

1. Open *WordPad*.
2. If it is not at its largest size then *Maximize button*.
3. Now click on the *Restore button*.

MOVING A WINDOW

Sometimes a window may be blocking your view and you wish to move it.

✓ *To move a window:-*

1. Position the mouse pointer anywhere along the title bar of the window.

2. Click and drag to the desired position.

TRY IT:

1. Start the *Program Note Pad*.
   (Make sure that the window is not at its largest size. If it is, *Restore* it.)
2. Move the window to the top left hand corner of the screen.

RESIZING A WINDOW

✓ *To change the size of a window:-*

1. Position the mouse pointer **along** any **border** of the window.

2. **When it changes to a double-headed arrow**, click and drag. You can only drag in the directions indicated on the arrow itself.

Example:-   ◄——►   This arrow indicates that you can only click and drag to the left or to the right.

↕   This arrow indicates that you can only click and drag up or down.

UNDERSTANDING THE MENU BAR

Earlier you were introduced to the menu bar. If you were to click on the different options on the menu bar, you would notice that a listing appears, highlighting the various features available within that particular option.

READING A MENU

Open *WordPad* again. Click on the word *File* which is on the menu bar. Notice a listing appears.

Some words have three dots after them, others do not (e.g. **New...**).

The following table highlights what you may see on a menu and their significance.

WHAT YOU MAY SEE ON A MENU	MEANING
Keyboard shortcut to the right of the command. *EXAMPLE:* **Save Ctrl + S**	Instead of the mouse, these keys can be used to activate that particular command. E.g. To save a file you can press the **<Ctrl>** key and the **<S>** key simultaneously .
• Checkmark *EXAMPLE:* ✓ **Ruler**	This means that the command is active. (In this example, it means that the **Ruler** is currently visible.)
• An arrow to the right of the command. *EXAMPLE:* **Picture ▶**	This means that more options are available. When you point to such a command, a secondary menu appears from which you can choose more commands.
• Three dots after a command. *EXAMPLE:* **Save As...**	When selected, a dialogue box will appear which contains more options. (A dialogue box is a small window.)

NOTE

In Microsoft Word2000, as you click on a menu item e.g. *File*, you may notice two arrow heads pointing downwards at the bottom of the listing that appears. ⋁⋁ This indicates that there are more items in the listing. If you point at this object, additional items in the listing will appear. This is important. You must always remember this.

UNDERSTANDING DIRECTORIES

WHAT ARE DIRECTORIES?

In order to understand what a directory is and to appreciate its usefulness, think of a secretary engaged in the task of filing documents. A secretary files documents so that they can be easily retrieved when they are needed. Therefore, she may have a file cabinet with drawers labeled A-C, D-F, G-I etc. Documents for clients whose surnames begins with B, for instance, will be placed in the drawer labeled A-C. Can you imagine the chaos that would result if she did not have such a method for classifying files? To find a particular document, she would practically have to search all the drawers!

The function of the directory is similar to that of the drawer. As the drawer stores the files of clients, so too the directory stores computer files. You will begin to see how useful this can be.

Suppose you are a teacher and you have prepared two Mathematics tests for your students. In addition to this, you have also developed a handout to give to your students on some of the concepts taught. To facilitate the easy location and retrieval of these files, it would be a good idea to put them in specific 'drawers' or directories. So the Mathematics test files could be placed in a directory called **Tests** and the handout files could be placed in a directory called **Notes**. This is illustrated in the diagram below:

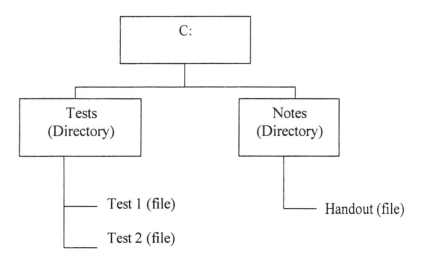

Notice that since the files and directories are stored on the *hard disk*, the diagram commences with a representation of the hard disk (C:). This is sometimes referred to as the *root directory*. (If the files were stored on the diskette, then the diagram would commence with 3½ Floppy A:)

So any time you wish to locate a Mathematics test you would head straight to the Test directory.

MORE ON DIRECTORIES

Now that you have grasped that concept, you are better able to understand more technical terms. From a directory, you can create a sub-directory. A sub-directory is a directory within a directory. To illustrate, recall the example previously given. As a teacher, you may need to prepare not only Mathematics but Science tests as well. To facilitate the easy retrieval of these files, it might be convenient to create two sub-directories **within** the main Test directory. These could be called **Mathematics** and **Science**. The Mathematics test files would then be stored in the Mathematics sub-directory and Science test files could be stored in the Science sub-directory. This is illustrated in the diagram below:

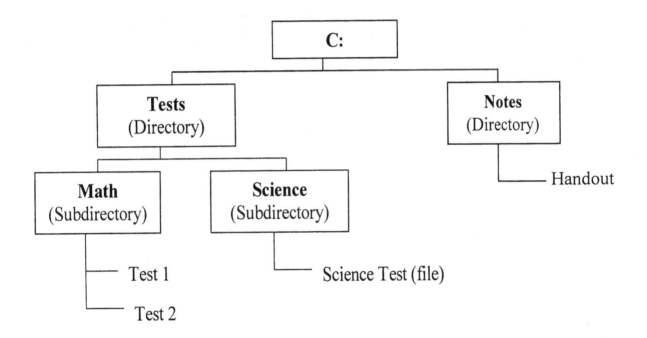

(In Windows another word is used which is synonymous to the word **directories**. It is **folders**. Both words will be used interchangeably.)

Directories = folders

9

WORKING WITH WINDOWS EXPLORER

Now that you have learnt what directories are, you must now learn to create, copy and rename them. You can do this by using *Windows Explorer*.

To start Windows Explorer simply:-

1. Click on **Start**.

2. Select **Programs**.

3. Move the mouse pointer to the secondary menu that appears and click on **Windows Explorer**. (A dialogue box appears).

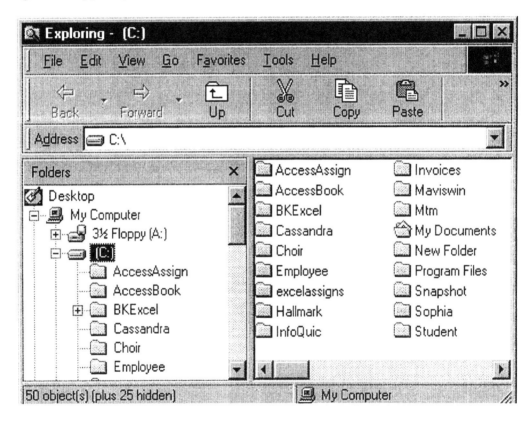

To create a new folder:-

1. In the left pane of the **Windows Explorer** window, click on the appropriate drive where you want to create the new folder. If creating the new folder on your diskette, select **A:** If creating it on your hard disk, select **C:** (Note, if you are creating the new folder on your floppy disk, you must first insert the disk in the floppy drive before clicking on the floppy drive **A:** in Windows Explorer.)

2. Select the *File* menu.

3. Click on the *New* command (a secondary menu appears).

4. Click on *Folder* from the secondary menu (The new folder appears in the right pane of *Windows Explorer* with a temporary name — *New Folder*).

5. Type in the name you intend for the folder.

6. Press the *Enter* key or *click* on a blank area within the window. The new folder is created and can be seen on the left pane of the Window.

NOTE

To view the contents of a folder, simply click on the folder in the left pane of the window and its contents will be displayed in the right pane of the *Windows Explorer* window.

CREATING SUB-DIRECTORIES

To create a sub-directory in Windows Explorer, click on the folder in which you want to create the sub-directory and then follow steps previously given for creating folders.

COPYING FILES OR DIRECTORIES

When you copy a file or folder, the file/folder remains at its current location and you store a duplicate of that file/folder at another location.

To copy a file or folder:-

1. Click on the *file* or *folder* you intend to copy.

2. Point to the *Copy* icon on the bar just below the menu bar, and click.

3. Select the *drive* (or *folder*) you intend to copy the file/folder to.

4. Point to the *Paste* icon and click.

Both the *Copy* and *Paste* icons can be found on the toolbar just below the menu bar.

MOVING A FILE OR DIRECTORY

When you move a file or folder, you actually remove it from its present location for storing at another location.

To move a file or folder:-

1. Click the *file* or *folder* you intend to move.

2. Point to the *Cut* icon and click.

3. Select the *folder* you wish to store the file or folder in. (This can be A:, C: or another folder).

4. Point to the *Paste* icon and click.

RENAMING FILES OR DIRECTORIES

At some time you may wish to change the name of a file or directory.

To rename a file or folder:-

1. Click on the *file* or *folder* you wish to rename.

2. Select the *File* menu.

3. Click on the *Rename* command.

4. Type the new name.

5. Press *Enter* or *click* on a blank area of the window.

SHUTTING DOWN

The process of turning off your computer is called shutting down. There is a procedure that must be followed when shutting down your computer.

To shut down:-

1. Click on the *Start* button.

2. Click on *Shut Down...* (A dialogue box appears).

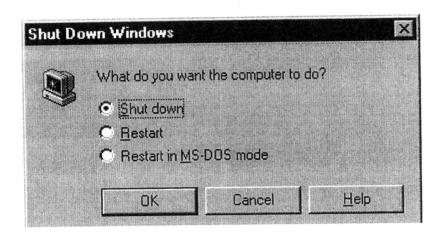

3. In the dialogue box that appears, select the option that indicates that the computer would be shut down.

4. Click on *Yes*.

5. Now wait until you see the words:-

It is now safe to turn off your computer.

• When those words are displayed, then you know for sure that you can safely turn off your computer system.

On some systems, these words may not appear, Instead, the system unit may shut down automatically. If this happens, all you need to do is turn off the monitor.

PRACTICE — EXERCISE 1 A

1. Create a directory on your floppy disk (A:): and name it **Employees**.

2. Create a directory on your hard disk (C:) and name it **Employers**.

3. Within the directory **Employees**, create two sub-directories and name one **Managerial** and the other **Clerical**.

4. Copy the sub-directory **Managerial** to the directory **Employers**.

5. Create a sub-directory within the directory **Employers** and name it **Wilsod Trading**.

6. Copy Willsod Trading to the directory **Employees**.

To confirm that you have done this exercise accurately, within **Windows Explorer**, click on the directory **Employees**. Three sub-directories should appear:- **Managerial, Clerical** and **Willsod Trading**.

Now click on the directory, **Employers**. The sub-directories **Managerial** and **Willsod Trading** should appear.

PRACTICE — EXERCISE 1 B

1. Create a directory on your floppy disk (A:) and name it **Customers**.

2. Create a sub-directory within **Customers** and name it **Professionals**.

3. Create a directory on your hard disk **(C:)** and name it **Engineers**.

4. Move the directory **Engineers** to the sub-directory **Professionals**.

5. Change the name of the directory **Customers** to **Clients** and sub-directory **Engineers** to **Surveyors**.

To ensure that you have done this exercise accurately, do the following:

Within **Windows Explorer**:-

• Click on 3¹/₂ Floppy **(A:)**. You should see the directory **Clients**.

• Click on **Clients**. You should see the **Professionals** sub-directory.

• Click on **Professionals**. You should see the **Surveyors** sub-directory.

• Click on your hard disk **(C:)**. The directory **Engineers** should not be seen.

CHAPTER 2

UNDERSTANDING THE BASICS

At the end of this chapter you should be able to:-

- Manipulate the following keys effectively:-
  CapsLock, Shift, Enter Spacebar.
- Use the keys Delete and backspace for the purpose of erasing text.
- Insert and delete blank spaces/ lines.
- Vary the location of the insertion point in a document.
- Create a new document.
- Open, save and close a file.
- Creating folders in Microsoft Word.
- Opening and saving files in folders.

Microsoft Word is a word processing application programme. Word processing programmes let you use your computer to compose and print letters, papers, reports and other types of documents. They offer more extensive editing capabilities than typewriters.

To start Microsoft Word:-

1. Click on *Start*.

2. Select *Programs*.

3. In the listing that appears to the right you should see *Microsoft Word*. Click on it.

THE MICROSOFT WORD WINDOW

When you start the Microsoft Word Program, some components of the window should be familiar to you.

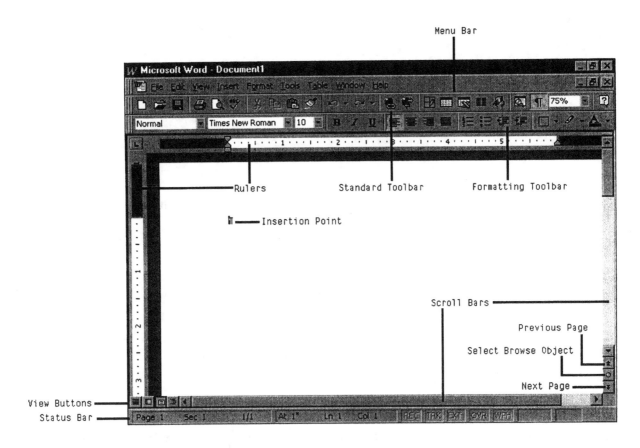

The *title bar* is at the top of the window. (In the title bar you should see the words **Microsoft Word** — **Document 1**). Below this you will see the *menu bar*. If you look carefully at the top right of the window, you should see the *Minimize, Restore* and *Close* buttons.

Directly below the menu bar are the *Standard* and the *Formatting* toolbars. Use the mouse to point at the various buttons on these bars. As you point at each button, a word appears indicating the function of that particular button. Later on, you will become more acquainted with these buttons.

Below the toolbars is the document window. In it, you will observe a short vertical line flashing continuously. This is called the *insertion point*. Any character typed, will appear at the precise position of the insertion point. (A *character* is any letter, number or symbol).

KEYBOARD BASICS

Before you go much further, you need to understand the function of some of the keys on the keyboard.

STANDING TYPING KEYS

These are the various keys such as letter keys, punctuation keys, space bar and format keys (Shift, Tab, Caps Lock).

ARROW KEYS

Arrow keys permit you to move around your document.

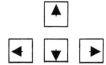

NUMBER KEYS

Number keys are grouped together to the right of the keyboard so that they are easier to use. To use these keys the *NumLock* light must be on. (At the top right hand corner of the keyboard is the NumLock light. Press the NumLock *key* to turn the light on or off).

Below the Number keys you would notice either a symbol or a word.

Example:

```
|   7   |
| Home  |
```

When the NumLock light is off, the key has a different function. It functions as the key indicated by the word(s) below the number on the Number key. In the previous example, if the NumLock light is off and this key is pressed, it will move the insertion point to the beginning of the line. (It functions as the Home key).

(Notice that apart from these Number keys, there are other keys on the keyboard that can be used to type numbers).

FUNCTION KEYS

These allow you to send commands to the software you are using. They provide shortcuts for doing routine tasks on your computer, (e.g. F6, F10).

SPECIAL KEYS

Special keys perform special tasks more efficiently. Exactly what the keys do depends on the software you are using. You can combine two or more keys to perform certain functions, (e.g. Alt, Ctrl).

Example:-

If you press <ALT>, keep it depressed and press **F**. This would activate the *File* menu.

ADDITIONAL INFORMATION

Notice that all the words on the menu bar have one letter underlined (e.g. _File_). If you press **<ALT>** and simultaneously press the letter underlined, it activates that particular menu.

KEYBOARD TIPS

KEYS	FUNCTION
<CAPS LOCK>	When pressed, the CAPS LOCK will come on. Any letters typed hereafter will be capital letters. Press the key again and the light will come off and the letters typed would be lowercase.
<SHIFT>	Press, <SHIFT> and a letter simultaneously, to display a capital letter. Press <SHIFT> and a key with two characters, (one above the other), to display the upper character.
ARROW KEYS	Use these keys to move the insertion point to any area on the screen.
<DELETE>	Deletes characters which appear to the right of the insertion point.
<BACKSPACE>	Deletes characters which appear to the left of the insertion point.
<END>	Moves the insertion point to the end of a line.
<HOME>	Moves the insertion point to the beginning of a line.
<CTRL> <HOME>	Moves the insertion point to the beginning of a document.
<CTRL> <END>	Moves the insertion point to the end of a document.
<PAGE UP>	Moves up one screen.
<PAGE DOWN>	Moves down one screen.

Now, try to type some words. Continue typing until you have at least two lines of text on the screen. (DO NOT press the **<ENTER>** key at any time). You should notice that as you type, when you reach the end of one line the text automatically moves to the next line. This is known as *wrapping* and it is advisable to always allow the text to wrap for itself when you are typing paragraphs. Do not press **<ENTER>** after each line unless it is necessary.

As you proceed, you will realize that you need a ***diskette***. A diskette is a device on which you can store your information. (Information can also be stored on your hard disk that resides inside your computer system unit). The computer recognizes the diskette as **A:** and the hard disk as **C:** Try to get a diskette as soon as possible.

SOLVING COMMON PROBLEMS

DELETING TEXT

The Backspace and Delete keys can be used to erase text.
Remember, this:-
* ***Backspace*** erases characters to the immediate ***left*** of the insertion point.
* ***Delete*** erases characters to the immediate ***right*** of the insertion point.

Both keys will erase characters one at a time.

INSERTING TEXT

Sometimes when typing, a word may be inadvertently left out. To make the necessary adjustment, we must first move the insertion point to the position where the word must be inserted.

 ✓ *To move the insertion point using the arrow keys:-*

Simply press the appropriate arrow keys to move the insertion point to the position desired.

The arrow key with the arrow pointing to the left, will move the insertion point to the left when pressed. The arrow key with the arrow pointing down, will move the insertion point down when pressed. etc.

To move the insertion point using the mouse:-

1. Position the mouse pointer at the point where the text must be inserted. The mouse pointer should have the shape of the letter I. (When the mouse pointer has this shape it is called the **I-beam**).

2. When the I-beam has been positioned at the point where the text is to be inserted, click. The insertion point will then be seen at that position.

3. **Now that you have moved the insertion point to the appropriate position, just type in the missing word.**

   In Microsoft Word 2000, you can position your insertion point anywhere within the document. This is known as the **Click and Type** feature. Just position the I-beam at the location where you want to start typing and double - click. The insertion point will move to that position.

INSERTING SPACE

Sometimes we need to include blank spaces within our document to make it more readable. Often beginners find this task challenging but it is really not that difficult.

To include a blank space in a document, first position your insertion point at the end of the previous paragraph. Then press the <ENTER> key. Keep pressing the <ENTER> key until you get the precise space required.

(There are other ways of accomplishing this task. This is just one suggestion.)

DELETING BLANK SPACES

To delete blank spaces, you have two options. Suppose you have two paragraphs separated by a blank space and you wish to combine both paragraphs to form one paragraph.

Option #1

1. Position your insertion point at the end of the first paragraph.

2. Keep pressing the **<DELETE>** key until both paragraphs are combined.

Option # 2

1. Position your insertion point at the beginning of the second paragraph.

2. Keep pressing the **<BACKSPACE>** key until both paragraphs are combined.

ONE WORD ON THE INSERT KEY

The **<INSERT>** key is used when you wish to overwrite text.

Example:-

Examine the sentence:- **This is a ship.**

Suppose you want an insertion point between **a** and **ship**.

If you wish to add the adjective **container** before the word **ship**, all you would have to do is to type the word **container**. (Remember, the insertion point is already positioned.)

Now, if you press the **<INSERT>** key before you begin to type, then , as you type, the word **ship** would be erased. You see the word **container** takes the place of the word **ship**. This is what is meant by the term **'overwrite'**. To deactivate this feature, you would need to press the **<INSERT>** key again.

CLOSING A FILE

In this book the words *file* and *document* will be used interchangeably. You close a document when you wish to cease working on the document.

To close a document:-

1. Click on the *File* menu.

2. Click on *Close*.

To exit Microsoft Word, click on *File* and then select *Exit*, or click on the *Close* button at the top right hand corner of the window.

CREATING A NEW FILE

Sometimes when you close a file you no longer see the insertion point and a grey screen is seen instead of the customary white document screen. When this happens it is an indication that you no longer have a document window open. Before you can type information onto a new document, you first have to create a new file. (In so doing you are creating a new document window.)

To create a new file in Microsoft Word:-

Simply click on the *New* button on the Standard toolbar.

OR

1. Click on *File* on the menu bar.

2. Click on the *New...* command. The New dialogue box appears.

3. Click on the *General* tab and activate *Blank document*.

4. Below the sub-heading *Create New* (on the bottom right hand side) activate *Document*.

5. Click on *OK*.

SAVING A FILE

When you save a file this means that it is permanently stored and that you can retrieve it whenever you desire. In the process of using Microsoft Word, you will need to save several files. Consequently, you need to find a way to distinguish between the files that are saved. This presents no problems at all. Files are given names during the 'saving' process.

When saving files, do not attempt to give two files the same name! If this is done the file that held the name originally, will be deleted and be replaced by the second file! Two files can have the same name only if they are stored in different directories.

To save a document on your diskette:-

1. Click on the *File* menu.

2. Click on *Save as...* (The *Save as* dialogue box appears).

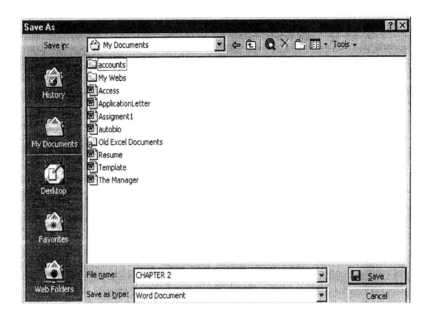

3. At the top left corner of the dialogue box, to the right of the words *Save in*, is the ***Drives drop-down list box***. A list box provides a listing of various options from which one must be selected. (This is the box where the words ***My Documents*** are currently displayed). Click the ***Drives drop-down list box*** arrow and select $3^1/_2$ **Floppy (A:)**. If you were saving the file on the hard disk you would select **(C:)**.

4. Towards the bottom of the dialogue box, look for *File <u>n</u>ame* and click in the ***File name*** text box. (This is the area where **CHAPTER 2** currently appears). Delete the text in the text box and type in the name you want for the file. (Usually names are chosen that help you to remember the contents of the file.)

5. Click on the ***Save*** command button on the lower right.

 NOTE WELL

Suppose you opened a document and made adjustments to it. Since the document already has a name, saving these additions is easy.

To save the changes that you have made:-

EITHER

1. Click on the *<u>F</u>ile* menu.
2. Click on *<u>S</u>ave*.

OR

1. Click on the **Save** button.

The ***Save <u>as</u>..*** option is only necessary when the file to be saved is a new file which **DOES NOT** have a name. If the file **already has a name** and you are simply making adjustments to it, just click on the ***Save*** button to save the changes made.

OPENING A FILE

You have typed a new document. You have saved it. You have closed it. Now you want to retrieve it so that you can make adjustments to it. So you need to open a file. Opening a file is easy. You just need to ensure that you are looking in the right place for the file (and you also need to know the name of the file).

There are many ways to open a *File*. Two of these ways are highlighted for you:-

1. Click on the *File* menu.

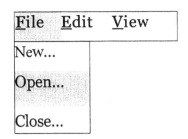

2. Click on *Open....*

   OR

3. Click on the *Open* button.

   The *Open* dialogue box appears.

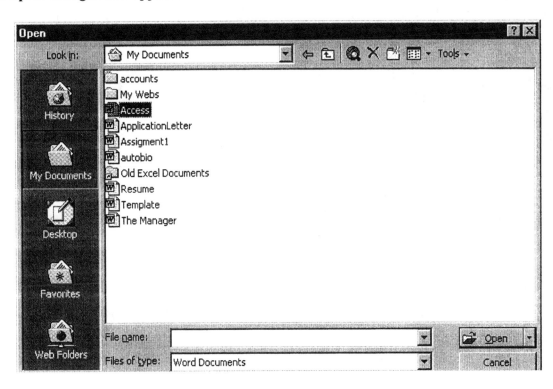

4. At the top left corner of the dialogue box, you should see the words *Look in*. Click in the list box to the immediate right of those words. (This is the area where *My Documents* is currently displayed).

5. Select $3^1/_2$ **Floppy (A:)** from the listing that appears. (This is how to specify that you want to open a file on the diskette). Now you should see all the documents saved on your diskette.

6. Click on the name of the file you want to open.

7. Click on the *Open* command button on the lower right.

FOLDERS

In Microsoft Word you can also create folders. Now you will learn how to create folders, save files in folders, and also open files that were saved in a folder.

CREATING FOLDERS WITHIN MICROSOFT WORD

To create folders:-

1. In the ***Open*** or ***Save as*** dialogue box, click on the ***Create New Folder*** button.

2. Type in the name you want to call the folder and press ***Enter***.

SAVING FILES IN FOLDERS

Having learnt how to create a folder, you need to learn how to save a file within a folder. However, before following the procedure outlined, you should note that in order to do this accurately, the file to be saved needs to be displayed on the screen and the folder must have already been created.

26

To save a file in a folder follow these steps:-

1. In the ***Save as*** dialogue box, select the drive that contains the folder in which you want to save the file. (If the folder is on your diskette, select **3¹/₂ Floppy (A:)** In the dialogue box, all the files and folders on the diskette will be displayed.

2. Select the ***folder*** and click on the the ***Open*** button.

3. In the ***File name*** box,type in the name you wish to give the file and click on the ***Save*** button. (Microsoft Word saves the file in the folder.)

OPENING FILES THAT ARE SAVED IN FOLDERS

To open a file saved in a folder:-

1. Select the ***File*** menu.

2. Click on the ***Open...*** command or click on the ***Open*** icon.

3. In the ***Open*** dialogue box select the drive that contains the folder in which the file is located, (e.g. **3¹/₂ Floppy A:**).

4. Select the folder that contains the file you desire to open.

5. Click on the ***Open*** button. (The name of the folder is displayed in the ***Look in:*** Box and a list of all the files in that folder appears below).

6. Select the file you want to open and click on ***Open***.

PRACTICE — EXERCISE 2A

1. On your diskette, create a directory called **Ex 1**.

2. On a new document, type the following information:-

─────────────── TO TYPE ───────────────

THE WORD PROCESSOR

Are you looking for a word-processing program? You need not look anymore because Microsoft Word is the program for you. Microsoft Word can be used to write letters, reports, keep notes, and organize ideas. In addition to creating text, you can insert pictures, charts and symbols.

─────────────── END OF TYPING ───────────────

---

3. Between the words **write** and **letters**, insert the word **professional-looking**.

4. Remove the words **keep notes** and symbols from your document.

5. Between the words **pictures** and **charts** insert the word **and**.

6. Remove the word **and** after the word **charts**.

7. Save the document in the directory **Ex 1** and give it the name **Exercise 2 A**.

PRACTICE — EXERCISE 2 B

1. Type the following text given.

```
───────────────────────── TO TYPE ─────────────────────────

WHY NOT HELP?


The Melloca will be having their annual fund-raising dinner at the Mellrose Hotel and Guest

House Ballroom on 25 August, 2000 at 7:00pm.  A contribution of $550 per person is re-

quested.  (The revenue will aid in the development of a home for street children).  Your usual

kind contribution will be greatly appreciated.  TOGETHER WE CAN DO IT!

───────────────────────── END OF TYPING ─────────────────────────
```

2. After the word **Melloca** insert the word **Social Club**.

3. Change **$550** to **$2500**.

4. Remove the words **per person** and replace it with **for adults and $1000 for children**.

5. Delete the sentence **Your usual kind contribution will be greatly appreciated**.

6. In its place, type **We need your support**.

7. **Save** the file in the directory **Ex 1** and give it the name **Exercise 2 B**.

8. **Close** the document.

PRACTICE — EXERCISE 2 C

1. Type the text given.

───── TO TYPE ─────

The advances in technology have enabled computers to provide numerous services for an ever-increasing number of people. Initially, a typical bank had a central computer centre that processed the data from various branches. Today, the clerk or teller enters transactions at once, via a terminal.

The terminal is connected to the computer that can access the files of customers' accounts. As a result, accounts can be queried and /or updated in a few seconds.

───── END OF TYPING ─────

---

2. Insert the heading **COMPUTERS AND BANKING** at the beginning of the document.

3. Insert the words **...One of the earliest uses of computers was in the banking industry** after the words, **... ever-increasing number of people**.

4. A line has been skipped between **once, via a terminal** and **The terminal is connected**. Remove this blank line so that it would be a continuous paragraph.

5. Skip a line between the sentence ending **...was in the banking industry** and the sentence beginning **Initially, a typical bank....**

6. Save the document as **Exercise 2 C**.

YOUR DOCUMENT SHOULD NOW LOOK LIKE THIS:-

COMPUTERS AND BANKING

The advance of technology has enabled computers to provide numerous services for an ever-increasing number of people. One of the the earliest uses of computers was in the the banking industry.

Initially, a typical bank had a central computer centre that processed the data from various branches. Today, the clerk or teller enters transactions at once via a terminal. The terminal is connected to the computer that can access the files of customers' accounts. As a result, accounts can be queried and/or updated in a few seconds.

PRACTICE — EXERCISE 2 D

1. Open the file saved earlier on your diskette called **Exercise 2 A**.

2. Erase the blank line space between the main heading and the passage below it.

3. Create a blank line between the sentence ending **"..Microsoft Word is the program for you."** and the sentence beginning **"Microsoft Word can be used..."** so that the second sentence begins a new paragraph.

4. Save the document as **Exercise 2 A A**.

1. Type the following passage in the box below.

──────── TO TYPE ────────

The inclusion of computers in education becomes significant and crucial only if it guarantees an enhancement of the learning process and results in superior accomplishment when compared to those obtained presently.

In infusing technology into teaching we must be assured that this will have a significant impact on students' performance.

──────── END OF TYPING ────────

---

2. Insert at the top of the document the heading **COMPUTERS IN EDUCATION**.

3. Place the insertion point immediately after the word **presently** and erase the word without repositioning the insertion point.

4. Place the insertion point at the beginning of the second paragraph and without changing the position of the insertion point, erase the blank line so that there is one continuous paragraph.

5. Insert the word **currently** after the word **obtained** in the first sentence.

6. Save the file as **key 1** *(Do not close the file)*.

7. Insert a blank line space between the first and the second sentences so that the second sentence begins a new paragraph.

8. Place the insertion point at the beginning of the passage and erase the words *The inclusion of* without changing the position of the insertion point.

9. Replace the common c in computers with a **capital** one.

10. Save the file as **key 2**.

CHAPTER 3

BASIC EDITING

At the end of this chapter you should be able to:-

- Block text.
- Underline, embolden and italicize text.
- Change the font and font size of text.
- Apply font effects to text.
- Change the case of text.

BLOCKING TEXT

"Blocking" is a way of selecting or choosing the text one wants to edit. It is a very useful technique for it helps you to perform certain tasks faster. You will see its usefulness shortly.
When text is blocked, **a black horizontal bar** appears over them.

There are several ways to block text.

METHOD 1

1. Move the *I-beam* to the beginning of the text you wish to block. (Remember when the mouse pointer changes to the letter I, this is called the I-beam.)

2. Press the left mouse button and keep it depressed while you drag the I-beam to the end of the text to be blocked.

METHOD 2

1. Position the insertion point at the beginning of the text to be blocked.

2. Hold down the **<SHIFT>** key and press the right arrow key on the keyboard. Keep the **<SHIFT>** key depressed and continue pressing the arrow key until all the text is blocked. (You can experiment by holding down **<SHIFT>** and pressing the other arrow keys to see the result).

METHOD 3

1. Position the *insertion point* at the beginning of the text to be blocked.

2. Position the *I-beam* at the end of the text to be blocked. (Do not move the insertion point).

3. Hold down the *<SHIFT>* key and click.

To remove the block, click anywhere in the document.

NOTE

While text is blocked, do not press any number keys or standard typing keys. If you do, your text will be deleted!

 USEFUL TIPS

To block a word:-   Position the I-beam within the word. Double click.

To block a line:-   Position pointer in the selection bar, at the same level of the line. Click once.

The selection bar is the area to the extreme left of the document where there is no text. This is denoted by the arrow. When using the selection bar for blocking, the arrow must slant to the right.

To block a paragraph:-   Double click in the selection bar.

To block the entire document:-   Click three times in the selection bar.

OR

Press <CTRL> and click in the selection bar simultaneously.

EMBOLDENING, ITALICIZING & UNDERLINING TEXT

Consider the following operations:-

<u>Underlining text</u>	(Self explanatory)
Italicizing text	Slanting text to the right
Emboldening text	Displaying text in bold letters

We will now learn how to achieve the above using Microsoft Word.

- ***To underline text***   Type text and block it.
  Click on the ***Underline*** button.

- ***To italicize text***   Type text and block it.
  Click on the ***Italicize*** button.

- ***To embolden text***   Type text and block it.
  Click on the the ***Bold*** button.

Instead of blocking text first, you can activate the buttons first and then type afterwards. The same effect will be achieved.

There are no restrictions on how many buttons can be activated at a time, Therefore, you can activate the ***Bold***, ***Italics*** and ***Underline*** buttons simultaneously.

REVERSING THE PROCESS

If you wish to ***remove*** the underline from the text:-

- Block the text.

- Click on the ***Underline*** button.

A similar procedure can be used to remove the ***Bold*** feature and the ***Italics*** feature.

1. Type the following in the same format as they appear. Take note of the format of the text displayed.

GOOD OR BAD?

Some people are of the opinion that <u>*a lot of television viewing*</u> *can have a* **negative impact** *on a* child's value system and mental prowess. Whether this is the case or not, *no one can deny that the television set* **has become the 'nanny' of many children** in several homes today.

---

2. Skip a few lines and type the following also:-

MICROSOFT EXCEL

Microsoft Excel is a *spreadsheet* program that allows you to :-

1)   **organize data.**

2)   complete calculations.

3)   *make decisions.*

4)   *graph* <u>*data*</u>.

5)   ***develop professional-looking reports.***

Save the file on your diskette as **Exercise 3 A**.

PRACTICE — EXERCISE 3 B

1. Type the short paragraph below:-

    Montreal. Canada's second largest urban area is Montreal. Montreal has a population of approximately 3.3 million people. The majority of the people speak French, but the city has always had a large English-speaking community.

2. Adjust the passage so that the word **Montreal** (which is at the beginning of the document), becomes the title of the document. (DO NOT RETYPE THE WORD).

3. Embolden and underline the heading **Montreal**.

4. Italicize the words **3.3 million people**.

5. Embolden, italicize and underline the words **speak French** and **English-speaking**.

6. Skip a line between the first and the second sentences so that the the second forms a new paragraph.

7. Erase the words **approximately** and **always had**.

8. Save the file as **Exercise 3 B**.

FONTS AND FONT SIZES

Fonts are the types of lettering you will find in a word processor. There are literally hundreds of them. They vary in appearance and size.

You can change the appearance of text by changing its font and font size.

Changing fonts — All of us have a different handwriting. Just as handwriting varies, so too the appearance of text can vary as well. When you change font you are changing the appearance of the text.

Example:- the words **font** and *font* are written in different fonts.

Changing font size — Changing the size of the text displayed.

Example: the words **font** and **font** are written in the same font but different font sizes.

To change fonts

1. Type the text and block it.
2. Click on the down arrow button next to the **Font** combo box.

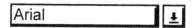

3. Select the font of your choice.

To change font sizes

1. Type text and block it.
2. Click on the down arrow button on the **Font size** combo box.

Select the font size of your choice.

Instead of blocking the text first before changing the font, you can also change the font first and then commence typing.

AN ALTERNATIVE METHOD

You can also change fonts and font sizes by using a different procedure:

1. Click on *Format* in the menu bar.
2. Select *Font...* (The Font dialogue box appears.)
3. Click on the *Font tab*.

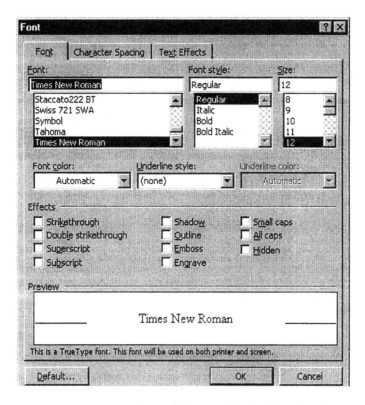

As you select your fonts, you can see a preview of the text by looking in the preview area.

*You may want to apply different underlining styles to text while in the **Font dialogue box** (e.g. double underline). To do so:-*

1. Ensure that the text is blocked.

2. Click on **Format** and **Font** and select the **Font tab**.

3. Click on the arrow in the list box under the word **Underline Style**:

4. Select the **Underlining** effect desired. (i.e. Double, Words Only etc.)

5. Click on **OK**.

*To remove the **Underline style**:-*

1. Block the text that has the underlining effect.

2. Select **Format** and **Font**.

3. Under the **Underline Style**: area, select **(none)**.

Within the font dialogue box you have several other useful options. We will focus on a few here and leave you to explore the others.

FONT EFFECTS

There are some other effects that can be accessed within the **Font** dialogue box. A few are explained below:-

Subscript   Lowers a character 3 points below the baseline and displays it in a smaller font size. (e.g. 8_2.)

Superscript   Raises a character three points above the baseline and displays it in a smaller font size. (e.g. 8^2.)

All Caps   Displays all letters as uppercase. (e.g. CHILDREN)

Small Caps   Displays all letters as uppercase. However, they appear smaller than they would have in **All Caps**. (e.g. CHILDREN)

To activate any of the features mentioned previously, first block the text that you want to apply the feature to, then:-

1. Click on *Format* and then *Font.*

2. In the dialogue box that appears, look in the area under the title *Effects* and select the desired option.

3. Click on *OK*.

You may need to deactivate the option afterwards. Remember you have to block the text first.

CHANGING CASE

Sometimes you may desire to change the case of the text that has already been typed. (e.g. you may want to display a word in capital letters instead of common letters).

To do so:-

1.   Block the text.

2.   Select *Format* on the menu bar.

3.   Select *Change Case...* (a dialogue box appears).

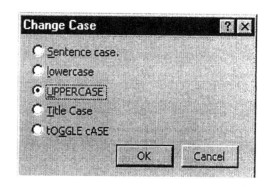

To change case you have to make a selection from among five options. Each is explained below.

Sentence case	Capitalizes the first letter of the first word in each sentence.
lowercase	The text blocked will be displayed in common letters.
UPPERCASE	All the text blocked will be displayed in capital letters.
Title Case	The first letter of each word blocked will be a capital letter.
tOGGLE cASE	Changes all uppercase letters to lowercase letters and all lowercase letters to uppercase letters.

4. Select the option of your choice.

5. Click on *OK*.

1. Type the following in the same format as they appear. Take note of the format of the text displayed.

   Take note of the fonts and font sizes in which the text must appear.

   HEADING:- font/font size — Tahoma, 14;   *PASSAGE: font/font size — Garamond, 14*

   ## SECONDARY STORAGE DEVICES

   Hard disks and **floppy disks** are *secondary storage devices*. Hard disks are more

   expensive than floppy disks. However <u>they</u> <u>can</u> <u>store</u> <u>more</u> <u>information</u>.

   ---

2. Skip a few lines and type the text that appears in the box below.

   HEADING:- Font /font size — Broadway, 16; ***PASSAGE:- Font /font size — CG Omega, 12***

   ## OPERATING SYSTEMS

   NO COMPUTER can function properly without AN OPERATING SYSTEM. Examples

   of operating systems are **Windows 98** and the **Disk Operating System** (DOS). These

   provide an interface (or form of communication between the *input devices and the*

   central processing unit.

   ---

3. Save the file on your diskette as **Exercise 3 C**.

1. Type the following in the same format as they appear. Take note of the format of the text displayed.

Font/font size of assignment below - Arial,11

FIVE WATERS COMPREHENSIVE HIGH SCHOOL

Academic Department

MATH TEST

<u>*Time: 30 mins.*</u>

SECTION A

<u>**Do all questions in this section. Show all working.**</u>

1.   *If x = 3 find the value of:-*

   a) x^2 b) $4x^2$ c) $2x^3 - 3x^2$

2.   **Find the value of the following:-**

   a) $23_8 + 216_{10}$ b) $275_8 + 11_{16}$

---

2. Save the file on your diskette as **Exercise 3 D**.

1. Type the following passage in the same format as they appear. Take note of the format of the text displayed.

Computers and Education

Since the early 1980s computers and computer software have been increasingly accessible to students and teachers in the classrooms, computer laboratories and school libraries. In 1995 there were about 4.5 million computers in elementary and secondary schools throughout the United States.

In Jamaica, there has been an increased effort to establish adequate computer laboratories at all schools. Presently, those students who do computer studies or information technology spend on the average, an hour per week using school computers. There are several ways in which computers can be used for teaching and learning in the classrooms, computer laboratories and school libraries. Some CD-ROMS and video disks electronically store thousands of articles, visual images, and sounds which enable students to browse through a maze of fascinating and visually appealing information.

Now that you have finished typing that passage, do the following:-

2. **Italicize** the first paragraph.

3. Before the second paragraph type in the sub-heading **Computers in the classroom**

4. Skip a line between **"...per week using school computers"** and **"There are several ways..."**

5. **Embolden, capitalize, italicize,** and **double underline** the main heading (Computers and Education).

6. Change the font of the main heading to **Tahoma**.

7. Change the font of the sub-heading to **Garamond**.

8. Change the font size of the main heading to **18**.

9. Change the font size of the sub-heading to **14**.

10. Change the font and font size of the **passage** (excluding the headings) to **Galliard BT** and **12** respectively.

11. Display the sub-heading in **small caps** and **underline it**.

12. Save the file on your diskette as **Exercise 3 E**.

PRACTICE -- EXERCISE 3 F

1. Open the file **Exercise 2 C**. (This file was created in Chapter Two).

2. **Double underline** the main heading.

3. Change the case of the main heading to the **title case**.

4. Capitalize all occurrences of the word **computer** in the passage.

5. Change the font of the heading to **Garamond** and the font size to **14**.

6. Change the font of the passage to **Arial** and the font size to **11**.

7. Italicize and apply the dot-dash underlining effect to the words *files of customer's accounts*.

8. Apply the small caps effect to words in the passage **THE ADVANCES IN TECHNOLOGY**.

TEST PREPARATION

In preparation for Self Test.1, the following passage must be typed in the same format as it appears below and saved as **Test 1 C**, as it will be needed for the exercise(s) that follow(s):-

---

the internet

The Internet Is The Fastest Growing Communications Medium Ever. With it, **educational** possibilities are endless. Bringing the **internet into classroom promotes educational** excellence and breathes new excitement and life into the educational experience. With the internet we can teach students to *search, retrieve, collect, and exchange* information. More importantly, they can learn to analyze, write about and then publish information on any topic. This cycle of <u>information gathering, analyzing, writing, and publishing</u> is important in the new information age already upon us.

SECTION A

Follow these instructions:-

a) Create a new directory on your diskette and name it **Self Test**. Then, create a sub-directory within **Self Test** and name it **Self Test 1**. **(2 Marks)**

b) Create a new document and type the short passage below:- **(4 Marks)**

Being an *adolescent* is an exciting <u>*time of life!*</u> You should try your best to enjoy it as much as possible.

Make the <u>**best**</u> of your *opportunity* to receive an <u>*education develop talents/skills and nurture new friendships.*</u> Unfortunately, it is at this time that some of us make mistakes that can affect us for life. Some youth engage in activities involving sex and drugs, among other things.

---

c) Insert the main heading **Being An Adolescent** at the top of the document. Embolden. capitalize and double-underline it. **(4 Marks)**

d) Skip two lines between the heading and the passage. **(2 Marks)**

e) There is a blank line space between the sentence ending **"...it as much as possible"** and the sentence beginning with **"Make the best...."** Delete the blank space so that you have one continuous paragraph. **(2 Marks)**

f) Delete the sentence beginning with the words : **"Some youth engage...".** **(1 Mark)**

g) Save the document as **Test 1 A** in the sub-directory Self Test 1. **(1 Mark)**

h) Remove the **bold** from the main heading and apply *italics* to it. **(2 Marks)**

i) Remove all <u>underlining styles</u> from the passage. **(2 Marks)**

j) Remove the italics from *"time of life"*. **Embolden** and <u>underline</u> it. **(2 Marks)**

k) Save the document as **Test 1 B** in the sub-directory Self Test 1. **(1 Mark)**

[Sub-Total   23 Marks]

SECTION B

Open the file **Test 1 C** on your diskette and follow the instructions below:

a) Change the case of the **first sentence** in the passage to Sentence case. **(2 Marks)**

b) Skip two lines after the sentence ending **"into the educational experience"** so that the following sentence begins a new paragraph. **(2 Marks)**

c) Remove the italics from the words **search, retrieve, collect and exchange.** **(1 Mark)**

d) **Double-underline** and apply **Small caps** to the main heading. **(3 Marks)**

e) Change the font and font size of the main heading to **Courier New** and **16** and of the passage to **Arial** and **11** respectively. **(2 Marks)**

f) Remove all underlining styles from the passage except the main heading. **(1 Mark)**

g) Capitalize all occurrences of the word **information** in the passage. **(2 Marks)**

h) Each occurrence of the word **educational** in the passage appears in bold letters. Remove the bold feature and underline each occurrence of the word. **(2 Marks)**

i) Save the file **Test 1 C** in the sub-head-directory **Self Test 1.** **(2 Marks)**

[Sub-Total - 17 Marks]

There should be three files saved on your diskette — Test 1A, Test 1 B and Test 1 C.

CHAPTER 4

BASIC FORMATTING

At the end of this chapter you should be able to :-
- Justify text and align text to the centre, right and left.
- Indent paragraphs.
- Insert and remove bullets and numbering.
- Set tab stops and tab leaders.
- Adjust the position of the bullets and text.
- Change line spacing.
- Insert columns in a document.

CHANGING TEXT ALIGNMENT

Alignment refers to the way the text lines up horizontally and vertically on the page. Microsoft Word is preset to align text left with the left margin, producing a ragged or uneven right edge. Thus when you start typing, the text normally appears on the left side of the document window first, and then proceeds to the right as you continue.

Text can be aligned in four different ways. Apart from aligning text to the left, text can be aligned to the right, centre and text can be justified.

These are the other three alignment icons.

	Align Right button	Align text right with the right margin, producing a ragged or uneven left edge.
	Centre button	Centres text on a page.
	Justify button	Adjusts text so that its right and left edges are not ragged but aligned with the left and right margins.

To align text, either:-

1.   Block text, then click on the appropriate alignment button (Left, Centre, Right or Justify)

        OR

2.   Click on the appropriate alignment button first, then type text.

USING THE TAB KEY

The **<TAB>** key can be very useful when you wish to indent text. (The **<TAB>** key is to the upper left of your keyboard).

To indent using the **<TAB>** key, just press the **<TAB>** key on your keyboard until the insertion point is at a position where you desire your text to be inserted. Then type. It is as simple as that!

You can eliminate the space created by the **<TAB>** key, the same way you delete characters, by using either the **<BACKSPACE>** or the **<DELETE>** key.

You also indent text by simply blocking it first and then clicking on the *Increase Indent* button or the *Decrease Indent* button on the *Formatting* toolbar.

Type the following résumé in the same format as it appears. Ensure that you **indent the text using the TAB key**. (The font of the entire document is **Garamond**. The font size of the girl's name is **26**, and the font size of the rest of the document is **12**). It would be wise to press **<ENTER>** at the end of each line instead of allowing the text to wrap automatically. Save the file as **Exercise 4 A**.

Lucy James

Address/Tel:-   14 John Lane, Spanish Town, St Catherine, Jamaica (984-1622)

Age:-   24

EDUCATIONAL ACHIEVEMENTS

1995 - 1998   *University of the West Indies, Mona Campus*

Bachelor of Science degree in Mathematics.

1987 - 1992   *St. Jago High School*

Obtained 3 A' Level passes in the following

subjects:- Mathematics, Physics, and History.

WORK EXPERIENCE

1992 - 1995   *Teacher*

NoWhere Basic School

EXTRA CURRICULAR ACTIVITIES   Football, netball

REFERENCES   Available upon request.

PRACTICE — EXERCISE 4 B

Type the following in the same format as it appears.

<u>**INTERNAL MEMORANDUM**</u>

TO: Daniel Lynch, Manager, Purchases and Inventory

FROM: Leroy Bennett, Manager, Sales and Marketing

DATE: 30 November, 1999

RE: **Weekly Output**

As per your request, please find below a schedule of the daily output over a four- month period. If you require any clarification please contact our department immediately.

<u>NUMBER OF UNITS OF OUTPUT</u>

	<u>Week 1</u>	<u>Week 2</u>	<u>Week 3</u>	<u>Week 4</u>
January	5245	5932	6090	6230
February	6123	6130	6250	6300
March	6080	6135	6310	6500
April	6155	6309	65809	6420

Save the file as **Exercise 4 B**.

PRACTICE — EXERCISE 4 C

Type the following in the same format as it appears.

A | Font – **Arial**   Font size - **11** |

INTERNAL MEMORANDUM

DATE:-   21/01/00
To:-   All Members of Staff
FROM:-   Inez Bradford, Academy Manager
SUBJECT:-   MONTHLY STAFF MEETING

Please be advised that our monthly staff meeting scheduled for Thursday, February 13 at 1:00 pm, has been postponed until further notice. This has been done to facilitate the participation of some members of staff in a seminar to be held at the Jamaica Conference Centre on the date.

B

> Font – **Times New Roman**
> Font size - **12**

Time	*Competitors*	*Judges*
9:30am.	Anthony Boguti Steve Harris Rick Wyman	R. Burnham S. Tracey
10:00am.	Ian Stange Sean O'Leary Topu Yan	B. Blackley
10:30am.	Lesley Farnham	R. Matthews

1. Change the font of the entire document to Colonna MT.

2. Change the font size to 18. (Adjust the names so that they are properly aligned).

3. Save the file as **Exercise 4 C**.

BULLETS

Bullets are small symbols that precede items in a list and allow you to itemize your points so that they are displayed with greater clarity. An example is given below:

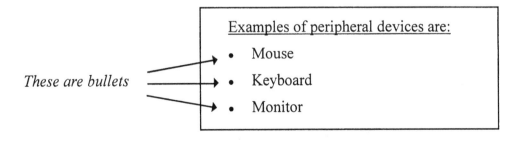

These are bullets

Examples of peripheral devices are:

- Mouse
- Keyboard
- Monitor

To insert standard bullets:-

1. Position the insertion point at the point that you want the bullet to appear.

2. Click on the ***Bullets*** button on the Formatting toolbar (to activate it). A bullet should appear.

3. Type text.

4. Press the **<ENTER>** key to move to the next bulleted item.

5. To end your bulleted list press **<ENTER>** <u>**twice**</u> after the final bulleted entry.

You can also type the text first, block it and insert the bullets afterwards by clicking on the ***Bullets*** button.

To remove bullets:-

1. ***Block*** the items you want to remove the bullets from.

2. Click on the ***Bullets*** button on the ***Formatting*** toolbar to deactivate it.

(Pictures can also be used in exactly the same way as the bullets. Just insert the picture and modify its size so that it becomes very small (the size of a bullet). Type your text and press <ENTER>. Another similar bullet should be automatically inserted directly below it in the next line.

NUMBERED LISTS

You can create numbered lists in your document the same way you create bulleted lists. It is easy!

To add standard numbers:-

1. Position the insertion point.

2. Click the ***Numbering*** button on the ***Formatting*** toolbar.

    (The ***Numbering*** button is normally next to the ***Bullets*** button.

You can also type the text first, block it, and click on the **Numbering** button on the toolbar. Normally when you select this button, numbers in the decimal number system appear (e.g. 1,2,3). Instead of this you may wish to use a, b, c, or i, ii, iii.

To insert a different numbering scheme:-

1. Position the insertion point (or block text).

2. Click on the **Format** menu.

3. Choose the **Bullets and Numbering...** command (The **Bullets and Numbering** dialogue box appears.)

4. Click the **Numbered** tab.

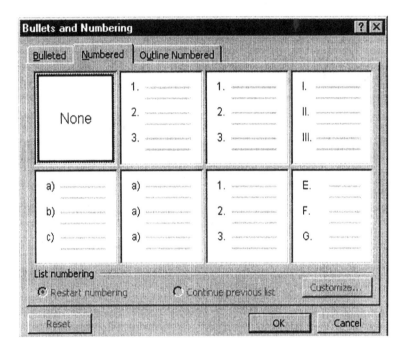

5. Select another numbering scheme.

6. Click on **OK**.

PRACTICE — EXERCISE 4 D

1. Type the following in the same format as it appears.

Font/font size - Tahoma, 14

How to learn about computers

1. Assume that you have the ability to learn how to use it.

2. Be curious.

3. Practise as much as possible.

4. Do not try to learn everything immediately.

5. If you have a problem, **DON'T PANIC!**

---

2. Save this as **Exercise 4 D 1**.

3. Now adjust your document so that it resembles the text below. (Do not retype the information!!)

How to learn about computers

• Assume that you have the ability to learn how to use it.

• Be curious.

• Practise as much as possible.

• Do not try to learn everything immediately.

• If you have a problem, **DON'T PANIC!**

Save it as **Exercise 4 D 2.**

ADVANCED METHODS OF FORMATTING

MORE ON BULLETS

Apart from the standard bullet •, there are other available bullets that can be selected.

To access other bullets:-

1. **Position** the insertion point at the point where the bullet is to be inserted (or block text).

2. Click on **Format** on the menu bar.

3. Choose the **Bullets and Numbering...** command. (A dialogue box is displayed).

4. Click on the **Bulleted** tab towards the top of the dialogue box.

5. Click on the type of bullet desired and click on **OK**.

Sometimes you may wish to adjust the distance between the text and the bullet.

To do so simply:-

1. Block the text and select **Format**. Select the **Bullets and Numbering...** command.

2. Click on the Bulleted tab at the top of the **Bullets and Numbering** dialogue box.

3. Click on the **Customize** button (the **Customize Bulleted List** dialogue box appears).

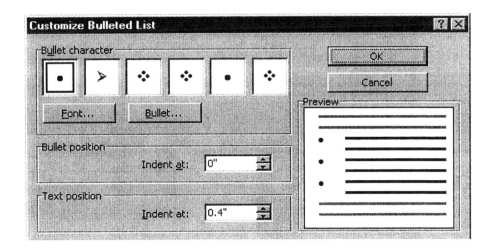

4. In the dialogue box that appears, make the necessary adjustments by setting the desired **Bullet position** and the **Text position**.

5. Click on **OK**.

PRACTICE — EXERCISE 4 E

Type the following in the same format as they appear.

Heading:	Font/font size:- Garamond, 18
Passage:	Font/font size - Times, 14
Bullet Position:	0.5", **Text Position:-** 0.75"

Productivity Software

Microcomputer-based *productivity software* is a series of commercially available programmes that can help people at home or workers in the business community save time and/or obtain information they require to make more informed decisions. Some of the most popular productivity tools available today in the marketplace include the following:

- ❖ Word processing
- ❖ Desk publishing
- ❖ Spreadsheet
- ❖ Database
- ❖ Graphics

Save the document as **Exercise 4 E.**

PRACTICE — EXERCISE 4 F

Type the following in the same format as they appear. Take note of the format of the text displayed.

Heading:	Font/font size:- Broadway, 18
Passage:	Font/font size - Galliard BT, 13
Bullet Position:	1.05", **Text Position:-** 1.75"

Categories of Computer Systems

All computers, irrespective of their size, have the same fundamental capabilities — *processing, storage, input, and output*. Five basic categories of computer systems are:-

      I.   Microcomputer system

      II.   Workstation

      III.   Minicomputer system

      IV.   Mainframe computer system

      V.   Supercomputer system

Save the document as **Exercise 4 F.**

Type the following in the same format as they appear. Take note of the format of the text displayed.

Heading: Font/font size:- Broadway, 22

Passage: Font/font size - Tahoma, 11

How do we use computers

The use of computers can be classified into several general categories, some of which are:-

1) Information systems/data processing

2) Personal computing. This can be used for a wide range of business and domestic applications, such as:

> ➤ Word processing software
>
> ➤ Desktop publishing software
>
> ➤ Spreadsheet software
>
> ➤ Graphics software

3) Science and research

4) Education

5) Entertainment

6) Artificial intelligence. There are four categories of artificial intelligence;

- Knowledge-based systems
- Expert systems
- Natural systems
- Robotics

Save the document as **Exercise 4 G.**

More on Indentation

Although we have touched on indentation in a previous lesson, there are still a few more things you need to learn. There are different types of indentations:-

- first line indent
- hanging indent
- left and right indentation

Examples:-

Today is Thursday and it is raining outside. There is a lot of traffic on the road as people hastily attempt to reach home before the showers become heavier.	Today is Thursday and it is raining outside. There is a lot of traffic on the road as people hastily attempt to reach home before the showers become heavier.	Today is Thursday and it is raining outside. There is a lot of traffic on the road as people hastily attempt to reach home before the showers become heavier.
First line indent	**Hanging indent**	**Left and right indentation**

Notice the graphic difference between the paragraphs.

(*Left and right indentation* allows you to set the distance of the text from the left and right margins.)

To set indents simply:-

1. Select the paragraph you desire to indent. (Block it or position the insertion point in the paragraph).

2. Select the *Format* menu.

3. Click on the *Paragraph...* command.

   (the *Paragraph* dialogue box appears).

4. Click on the *Indent and Spacing* tab

   at the top of the box.

5. To choose either the *first line indent* or the *hanging indent*, go to *Special*: and select the option from its drop-down list box. Otherwise set the required indentation spacing in the *Left* and *Right Indentation* list boxes.

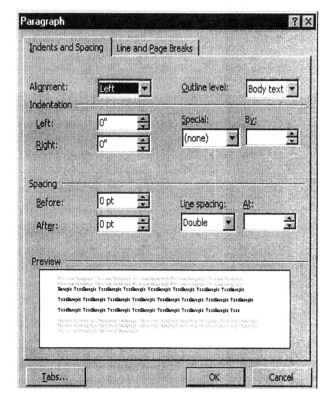

6. Click on *OK*.

(Type the paragraph given in the example, and indent it using the three types of indentations. The left and right indentations should be set at 3". In order to use this feature, you must allow the text to wrap automatically when typing the paragraphs).

SETTING TAB STOPS

When you press the <TAB> key or click on the *Increase Indent* button, the insertion point moves to the next tab stop which is normally set at 0.5 inches. (By tap stop we refer to the distance the insertion point travels when the <TAB> key is pressed). You can modify the tap stop position/measurement as you desire. In other words, you can change the distance travelled when the tab key is pressed from 0.5 inches, to any other reasonable measurement.

To set the tab stop:-

1. Click on the *Format* menu.

2. Select the *Tabs...* command (The *Tab* dialogue box appears).

3. Modify the default Tab stop by using the up or down arrow to set the new tab stop desired.

4. Click the *Clear* button. This clears the *text box below the heading *Tab Stop position*.

5. Type in the the new tab stop measurement in the text box below *Tab Stop position*.

6. Click on the the *Set* button and click on *OK*.

TABS WITH LEADERS

Tab leaders are solid, dotted or dashed lines that fill the space left by the tab key when it is pressed. They are useful when creating a **Table of Contents**, for example, as it helps the reader identify the pages on which certain information can be obtained.

Example:

INTRODUCTION .... Page 1

CHAPTER .... Page 4

To specify the Tab leader:-

1. Select *Format* and *Tabs*.

2. Click on the leader desired in the *Tab* dialogue box.

3. Set the Tab stop position. (The Tab stop position selected, is the <u>distance travelled</u> when the tab key is pressed. The leader characters appear up to this point).

4. Select *Set* and click on *OK*.

To reset your tab settings:-

1. Select *Format* and *Tabs*.

2. Select *Clear All*.

3. Type in the desired Tab stop position.

4. Click on *OK*.

PRACTICE — EXERCISE 4 H

Type the following in the same format as they appear. Take note of the format of the text displayed. Follow the instructions in the box below.

```
Font - Arial
Font size of heading - 16
Font size of rest of document - 11
Tab stop position - 5"
```

Table of Contents

Save the file on your diskette as **Exercise 4 H**.

Type the following in the same format as they appear. Take note of the format of the text displayed. Follow the instructions in the box below.

---

1) **Set** the left and right indent options for the first paragraph to **0.5"**.

2) For the three bulleted paragraphs, set the bullet and text position as follows:-
   Bullet position - 1.5" and **Text position - 1.75"**.

3) The three bulleted paragraphs must be left and right indented at **1.5"**.

4) **Font/font size of passage:** Times New Roman, 12.

5) **Font/font size of Heading:** Times New Roman, 20.

MICROSOFT POWERPOINT

Microsoft PowerPoint offers to the user **five** different views in which to create, change and show presentation. Each view offers a different way of looking at the presentation. We now examine three of the five views.

❖ **Slide** view displays one slide one at a time and enables all operations for that slide. You can enter, delete or format text.

❖ **Slide sorter** view displays all the slides in the presentation on one screen. In this view you can delete, move or copy slides.

❖ **Outline** view shows the presentation in outline form. No pictures are displayed only text. This is the fastest way to enter or edit text in a presentation.

Save as **Exercise 4 I** and **close it**.

CREATING COLUMNS

You can format your document so that you have two or more columns of text appearing within a page.

To do so, simply:-

1. Select the *Format* menu.

2. Select *Columns...* (The *Columns* dialogue box is displayed).

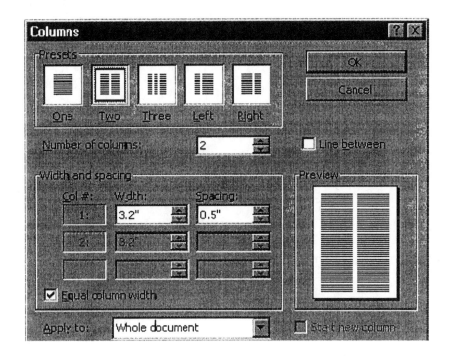

3. Under *Presets*, select the type of column setup (or set the number of columns you desire in the *Number of Columns* box (i.e. 3,4 etc).

4. Activate the *Line between* check box if you wish to print a vertical line between the columns.

5. If you desire each column to have equal width then activate the *Equal Column Width* check box.

6. In the *Apply to:* list box, select whether you want to apply this format to the entire document or whether you want to apply this format from the point where the insertion point is, onward.

7. Click on *OK*. Now you can type.

PRACTICE — EXERCISE 4J

In preparation for the exercise below, the following passage must be typed in the same format as it appears and saved as PROPOSAL, as it will be needed for the exercise that follows:-

INTRODUCTION

For several years now the portion of the canal specified under the heading **Work Area** has not been cleaned or repaired. We therefore bring this to your attention and propose to clean same. The canal needs to be cleaned and repaired because there are several problems associated with a blocked and damaged canal:-

DRAINAGE. The canal does not provide proper drainage. Water accumulates and creates unnatural pools, which can lead to flooding and possibly death.

PUBLIC HEALTH. It contains cracks, holes and cans from garbage, in which water settles and results in the breeding and spreading of mosquitoes.

ASCETICS. A dilapidated gully brings down the general look of the community. We want the citizens to have a certain level of pride in their community.

WORK AREA

Canal beginning at Demshire Avenue and ending at Viewmount Crescent.

REPAIR WORK

This involves:-

Repairing cracks and pot holes at the side and bottom of the canal.

Clearing bushes

Removing and cleaning debris and other obstacles that impede the smooth flowing of water.

Debris will be removed from both the side and bottom of the canal.

Equipment and Material

Manpower/labour

30 men will be required to complete the work in 7 days.

SUMMARY

The cleaning and repairing of the canal will provide employment for some.members of the community, improve the general outlook of the community and aid in national pride and community development.

You are required to:-

1. Retrieve the file **PROPOSAL** that was saved on your diskette.

2. Format the file in **two newspaper style columns**.

3. Insert the title **A healthier community** at the top of the document.

4. **Embolden** and **capitalize** the title.

5. Below the heading **Equipment and Material** add the following:-

	Unit Price	Extended Price
5 machetes	$120.00	$600.00
6 hoes	$540.00	$3240.00
3 pairs water boots	$720.00	$2160.00
3 hammers	$250.00	$750.00

6. Between *Machetes* and *Hoes* add the following:-

   5 Push-brooms $160.00 $800.00

7. **Insert** bullets to itemize each repair work below the heading **Repair Work**. The Text position should be **0.55-inch** and the Bullet position **0.25 inch**.

8. The following headings **(Equipment and Material, Manpower/Labour and Summary)** should be **bolded, double-underlined** and placed in **small caps**.

9. Save the document as **Exercise 4 J**.

PRACTICE — EXERCISE 4 K

1. Open the file on your diskette called **PROPOSAL**.

2. Enter the title that follows at the top of the document:- **Demshire Gardens: A healthier Community**.

3. Change the font and font size of the title to **Garamond** and **16** respectively.

4. **Embolden, italicize** and apply the **Small caps** effect to the title.

5. Format the content of the file in **three newspaper style** columns (**Note**, the columns should begin after the title).

6. The passage should be in a smaller font than the title.

7. Remove the **Small caps** effect from the sub-headings and **embolden** and **underline** them.

8. Insert numbers to itemize each repair work below the sub-heading **Repair Work**. The Numbered position should be **0.05"** and the Text position **0.35"**.

9. Save the file as **Exercise 4 K**.

PRACTICE — EXERCISE 4 L

INSTRUCTIONS - Type the following in the same format as they appear. Take note of the format of the text displayed.

Note:- Use **double** line-spacing
Font and **font size** of title — **Americana BT, 16**
Font and **font size** of rest of passage — **Garamond, 12**

Disasters - Must We Expect Another?

As this century rapidly comes to a close, more **natural disasters** threaten to make this year, 1999, the one in which most lives were lost due to catastrophic events. Earlier in the year we heard of hurricanes, floods, earthquakes, and typhoons. Now *Venezuela* is experiencing its share of pain and misery as it struggles to come to terms with the mud slide that, according to estimations, has killed 30,000 people and left 250,000 **homeless**.

LOS CORALES was one of the worst hit areas in the worst disaster in Venezuela this century. Authorities most likely will be unable to recover all the bodies which are buried under a 3-metre deep pile of boulders, dirt and trees. **President Hugo Chevaz** says he may have to declare the site and other disaster areas like it *'MEMORIAL GROUNDS'*. There are just a few more days left in this year. One wonders if we can expect anymore disasters or whether *our eyes can remain dry a bit longer*.

Test Preparation

In preparation for **Self Test 2**, teachers are required to type the passage below in the same format as it appears and save the file as **Test 2**. Then copy the file to the students' diskettes.

(Main heading) input/output devices

Programs and data <u>must</u> be entered into ***memory*** for processing, and the results obtained from processing <u>must</u> be recorded or displayed. ***Input devices*** are used to enter data into ***memory*** for processing, while ***output devices*** display the results obtained from processing. Below is a list of some common ***input/output devices:-***

(Sub-heading) Input/output processor

Instead of having each interface communicate with the *central processing unit*, a computer may incorporate one or more external processors and assign them the task of communicating directly with all ***input/output devices***. Each *input/output* processors takes care of input and output tasks, relieving the central processing unit of the task of *input/output* transfers.

Self Test 2

Instructions:-

a) Within the **Self Test** directory (which should be on your diskette),
    create a sub-directory called **Self Test 2**.   **(1 Mark)**

b) Change the file **Test 2** on your diskette.

c) Change the font of the main heading to **Allegro BT** and the font size to **20**.   **(1 Mark)**

d) Capitalize the main heading and apply **Title case** to the sub-heading.
    Remove the double underline from the headings.   **(3 Marks)**

e) Set the **Left** and **Right** indent options for the first paragraph to **0.7-inch**.   **(2 Marks)**

f) Apply the **First-line** indent option to the paragraph immediately below the sub-heading **(Input/output processor)**, and set it **1-inch** from the left margin.   **(2 Marks)**

g) Insert the following list of input/output devices at the end of the first paragraph:-

Mouse & trackball

Keyboard & scanner

Joystick & fax modem

Printer and monitor

(2 Marks)

h) Apply bullets of your choice to the list of input/output devices(inserted above). Indent the bullets at **1-inch** and the text at **1.05 inch** from the left margin.   **(2 Marks)**

i) Italicize all occurrences of the word **processing**.   **(2 Marks)**

j) Save the file as **Test 2 A** in the sub-directory **Self Test 2**.

k) Apply **Small caps** to all occurrences of the term **input/output devices** in the passage.   **(2 Marks)**

l) Delete the words **Main-heading** and **Sub-heading** from the file.   **(1 Mark)**

m) **Justify** the passage and **centre** headings.   **(2 Marks)**

n) Remove all superscript and subscript effects from the document.   **(2 Marks)**

o) Remove the bullets from the **list of input/output devices** and replace them with numbers (i.e. 1,2,3). Indent the numbers at **1.35-inch** and the text at **1.6-inch** from the left margin.   **(3 Marks)**

p) **Save** the file as **Test 2 B** in the sub-directory **Self Test 2**.

[Total - 25 MARKS]

At the end of this assignment you should have two files saved in the **Self Test 2** sub-directory:- **Test 2 A** and **Test 2 B**.

CHAPTER 5

WORKING WITH PAGES

At the end of this chapter you should be able to:-

- Change line spacing.

- Change page margins.

- Change page orientation.

- Preview and print a document.

- Insert/remove page numbering.

- Insert headers and footers.

- Insert footnotes and endnotes.

- Insert/delete page/selection breaks.

CHANGING LINE SPACING

You are typing an official document and it is recommended that you use double line spacing. What are you going to do? This is not difficult at all.

To change line spacing:-

1. Block the paragraph.

2. Click on the *Format* menu.

3. Select *Paragraph* (The *Paragraph* dialogue box appears).

4. Select the *Indent and Spacing* tab at the top of the dialogue box.

5. Under *Line Spacing* select the type of spacing desired (i.e. Single, double etc.)

6. Click on *OK*.

CHANGING MARGINS

A page has four margins — top, bottom, left, right. These control the distance of the text from the top of the page, the bottom of the page, the left of the page and the right of the page, respectively.

To set page margins:-

1. Click on *__File__* on the menu bar.

2. Select *Page Set-up...* (The *Page Set-up* dialogue box appears). Click on the *Margin* tab at the top of the dialogue box.

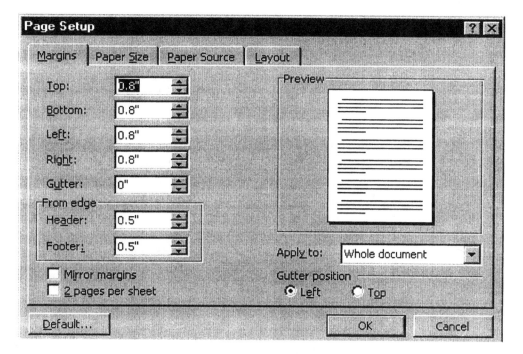

3. Adjust the left and right margins, and the top and bottom margins, by clicking on the appropriate arrows. (The *Preview* area displays the impact of these adjustments on your document).

4. Click on *OK*.

CHANGING PAGE ORIENTATION

There are two ways a document can be printed:-

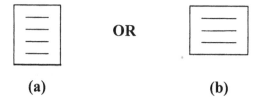

       (a)   **(b)**

The first **(a)** is called **portrait**. The second **(b)** is called **landscape**. For most computer systems the default orientation is portrait.

If you desire to change the orientation, this is what you do:-

1. Select *File* from the menu bar.

2. Select *Page Set-up*.

3. Click on the *Paper Size* tab.

4. Under *Orientation*, select either portrait or landscape.

5. Click on *OK*.

PRINT PREVIEW

It is always advisable to get a preview of your document before you print it. This is one way to ensure that it is properly formatted and has an appropriate layout on the page. The Print Preview feature allows you to view what your document would look like when it is printed.

To get a print preview:-

1. Open the document.

2. Click on the *Print Preview icon*.

You can control viewing size of the document by clicking on the **Zoom Control** combo box and selecting the desired percentage. If all the pages of your document are shown, the scroll bars can be used to bring them into view. To return to the normal view of your document, simply click on the **Close** button.

PRINTING

Printing is easier than you think.

To print a document:-

1. Open the document.

2. Click on the **Print icon**.

If you desire specific pages to be printed, or more than one copy of the document, instead of clicking on the Print icon:-

1. Select **File** from the menu bar.

2. Select **Print**. (A dialogue box appears).

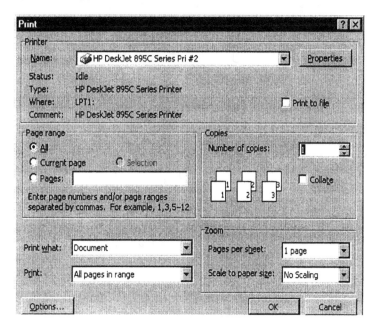

In the dialogue box which appears, you can:-

1. Indicate how many copies you desire.

2. Indicate the pages to be printed (Under **Page Range** select **Pages**. In the textbox, type in the pages you wish to print, separating each with a comma. Otherwise type in a range i.e. 1-3.)

Lastly, click on *OK*.

If you desire to print a specific page, you can simply place the insertion point in the page and then, in the *Print* dialogue box under *Page Range*, select *Current page*. Then click on *OK*.

PRACTICE — EXERCISE 5 A

1. Open the file **Exercise 3 E** (Created in Chapter 3).

2. Change the margins to **0.7"** on the left, right, top and bottom.

3. Change the line spacing to **Double**.

4. Change the page orientation to **Landscape**.

5. **Justify** the passage.

6. Change the font of the **entire** passage (including the heading) to **Courier New**.

7. Apply the **First line** indentation option to both paragraphs.

8. Apply the **Small caps** effect to the heading and **double-underline** it.

9. Obtain a preview of the document and print it.

10. Save the document as **EXERCISE 5 A**.

PRACTICE — EXERCISE 5 B

1. Open the file **Exercise 4 E** (Created in Chapter 4).

2. Change the bullets to numbers(For example, 1,2,3,...).

3. Adjust the Numbered position to **0"** and the Text position to **0.25"**.

4. Change the page orientation to **Landscape**.

5. Change the left and right margins to **1.9"** and the top and bottom to **1.7"**.

6. Apply the **Small caps** effect to the heading and **centre** it.

7. Change the line spacing to **1.5 lines**.

8. Obtain a preview of the document and print it.

9. Save the document as **Exercise 5 B**.

PRACTICE — EXERCISE 5 C

1. Open the file **Exercise 4 F** (created in Chapter 4).

2. Apply the **First line** indentation option to the first paragraph and set it at **0.8"**.

3. Change the page orientation to **Landscape**.

4. Change the line spacing to **double**.

5. Change the margins to **2"** all around.

6. **Capitalize** and **centre** the heading.

7. Change the numbered items to bulleted items and set the Bullet position and the Text at **0.4"** and **0.65"** respectively.

8. Obtain a preview of the document and print it.

9. Save the document as **Exercise 5 C**.

INSERTING PAGE NUMBERS

At some point, you may wish to insert page numbers into your documents. To do so, just follow the steps given.

To insert page numbers:-

1. Click on the ***Insert*** menu.

2. Select ***Page Numbers***. (The ***Page Numbers*** dialogue box appears).

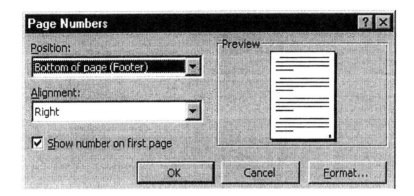

3. Select the position where you want the numbers to appear (i.e. top or bottom).

4. Also select the alignment of the numbers (i.e. right, centre or on the left).

5. Click on **OK**.

*Sometimes you do not want the first page of your document to be numbered. If that is the case, then on entering the **Page Numbers** dialogue box:-*

1. Deactivate the **Show number on first page** check box by clicking on it.

2. Click on the **Format** button on the right corner of the window. (Another dialogue box appears).

3. Under **Page Numbering**, select the **Start At** option button and ensure that **0** is displayed. The first page is numbered 0. However 0 will not be displayed on the page as you have deactivated the check box next to **Show number on first page**. The second page will be numbered as page number 1. This page number will be displayed. (If you wanted your first page to start with a number other than 1, you would enter that value in the **Start At** text box).

4. Click on **OK**.

REMOVING PAGE NUMBERS

To remove page numbers:-

1. Double-click on any page number. (The **Header and Footer** toolbar appears).

2. Block the number and press **<DELETE>**. All the page numbers will be deleted.

3. Click on the Close button on the *Header and Footer* toolbar.

It is that simple.

HEADERS AND FOOTERS

A *header* is the same text appearing at the top of every page while a *footer* is the same text appearing at the bottom of every page. When you type the desired *header* or *footer once*, it is automatically inserted on each page of the document.

To create a header:-

1. Select *View* on the menu bar.

2. Choose the *Header* and *Footer* command. (The *Header* and *Footer* toolbar appears. You will also notice that the *Header* area is outlined and *Footer* area is outlined.)

3. To create a *Header*, type text in the *Header* area outlined. (You can click on the *Switch Between Header* and *Footer* button to move between the Header area and the Footer area.)

4. Click the *Close* button.

The text typed would now appear at the top of each page in your document.

To create a *Footer*, follow the same procedure (except you would type in the Footer area).

To create different headers or footers for odd and even pages:-

1. Click on *View* menu.

2. Select *Header and Footer*. The *Header and Footer* toolbar appears.

3. Click on the *Page Setup* tab on the toolbar.

4. In the dialogue box that appears, click on the **Layout** tab.

5. Select the *Different odd and even* check box and then click on *OK*.

6. To create a header for all even pages, type in the *Even Page Header* area. (To create a footer

for all even pages, type in the *Even Page Footer* area. To create for all odd pages, type in the *Odd Page Header* area).

7. Click on the *Close* button on the *Header* and *Footer* toolbar.

FOOTNOTES AND ENDNOTES

A *footnote* is used in a document or book to give information on the source of quoted material. A reference number appears immediately after the quote in the text, and a corresponding footnote number or symbol appears at the bottom of the same page.

An *endnote* contains the same information as a footnote but appears at the end of a section or at the end of a document or book.

To insert a footnote or endnote:-

1. Position the insertion point where the footnote or endnote is to be inserted.

2. Select the *Insert* menu.

3. Choose the *Footnote* command. (A dialogue box appears.)

4. Select either the *Footnote* or *Endnote* option.

5. Click on *OK*.

The insertion point immediately jumps to the bottom of the page so that you can type in the source of your material.

To delete the footnote or endnote, select the footnote reference number that is within the document and press <DELETE>.

PAGE BREAKS

PROBLEM! You are typing a document and you want to type just a few lines on one page and then type the other lines on a second page. The problem is, how do you get the insertion point to the second page so that you can continue typing? Do not be daunted by this. It is no problem at all!

Normally, you would press the <ENTER> key continuously until the insertion point reaches the second page. But there is an easier way. You can insert a **page break**. When you insert a page break, the insertion point is immediately repositioned on a new page.

To insert a page break:-

1. Select the *Insert* menu.

2. Select *Break*.

3. In the dialogue box that appears, select *Page Break*.

4. Click on *OK*.

SECTION BREAK

Section breaks can be very useful. To illustrate, let us say that you created a document, and wanted to number the first three pages using Roman numerals,and the other pages using the decimal number system (the one we normally use). In order to accomplish this, you could insert a **Next Page section break** at the bottom of the third page. This permits you to use different numbering techniques for the pages before and after the section break.

To insert a section break:-

1. Place the insertion point where you want to insert the Section break.

2. Click on the *Insert* menu and select *Break*. (The *Break* dialogue box appears).

3. Under the heading *Section break types*, select the appropriate and click on *OK*.

Section break types	*Functions*
NEXT PAGE	Inserts a section break and starts the new section on the next page.
CONTINUOUS	Inserts a section break and starts the new section on the same page.
ODD OR EVEN PAGE	Inserts a section break and begins the new section on the next odd or even-numbered page.

DELETING BREAKS

1. Select the *break* you are desirous of deleting.

2. Press the *Delete* button on the keyboard.

PRACTICE — EXERCISE 5 D

1. Open the file **Exercise 4 I** which is stored on your diskette (created in Chapter 4).

2. Insert a **Page break** after the first paragraph and between each bulleted paragraph.

3. **Number** these pages. (You should have four pages).

4. Set all **margins** at 1".

5. Change the **page orientation** to landscape.

6. Change the **line spacing** to 1.5 lines.

7. Change the **page numbers** to Roman numerals (i.e. I, II, III etc.).

8. Insert a **footer** in your document that bears the following words:

    Edited by [Name]   (Type your name in place of [Name])

    (When you have inserted this footer, it should appear on all pages).

9. Insert a **footnote reference number** at the end of the first sentence of this document (i.e. the sentence that begins **Microsoft Power Point offers to the user.....**).

    At the bottom of this page type: **All about Computers, page 12**

10. Obtain a preview of this document and if you have a printer:-

    *   Print page 1 only.

    *   Print pages 2 to 4.

    *   Print page 1 and page 3.

11. Save the file as **Exercise 5 D**.

PRACTICE — EXERCISE 5 E

1. Open the file **Exercise 4 C** (created in Chapter 4).

2. Insert a **Continuous section break** immediately below the paragraph ending "**... on the same date**".

3. Change the margins above the Section break to **0.7"** (Top and bottom) and **1.5"** (left and right).

4. Change the line spacing above the Section break to **1.5 lines**.

5. Change the margins below the Section break to **1.25"** all around.

6. Change the line spacing below the Section break to **double**.

7. Insert the header in your document:- **For office use only**.

8. Obtain a preview of your document and print it.

9. Save the document as **Exercise 5 E**.

PRACTICE — EXERCISE 5 F

1. Open the file **Exercise 3 E** on your diskette (Created in Chapter 3).

2. Insert a **Next page section break** immediately below the first paragraph which is above the sub-heading **COMPUTERS IN THE CLASSROOM**.

3. Change the left and right margins above the Section break to **1.6"**.

4. Change the line spacing above the Section break to **double**.

5. Number both pages using the numbering format **I, II**.

6. Insert the header at the top right-hand corner of the document:- **Technology News**.

7. Change the font and font size of all the paragraphs (Excluding the headings) to **Tahoma** and **13** respectively.

8. Change the line spacing below the Section break to **1.5 lines**.

9. Change the left and right margins to **0.8"**.

10. Insert the footer:- **Technology, The Agent Of Change**.

11. Save the document as **Exercise 5 F**.

CHAPTER 6

NECESSARY TOOLS

At the end of this lesson you should be able to:-

• Find and replace text.

• Cut, copy and paste text.

• Collect and paste text.

• Check the spelling in a document.

FIND AND REPLACE TEXT

Sometimes you may need to find specific words within your document. There is a very useful feature that can do that for you.

To find a word or words in your document:

1. Click on the *Edit* menu.

2. *Select Find.*

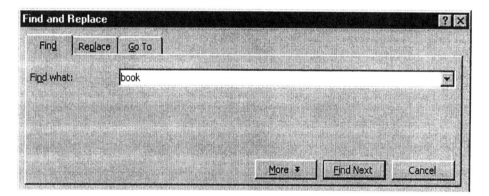

3. In the dialogue box that appears, type in the word you wish to find in the *Find What* text box that appears.

4. Click on the *Find Next* button.

Sometimes you not only want to find a word but you want to replace it with something else.

To do so:-

1. Click on *Edit.*

2. Select *Replace.* A dialogue box appears.

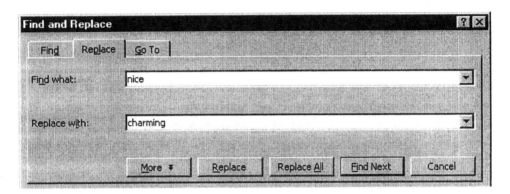

3. Two text boxes appear. In the *Find What* text box type in the word you want to replace.

4. In the *Replace With* text box, type in the word that should replace the word typed in step 3.

5. Now you have an option. You can either replace all occurrences of the word typed in step 3, or find the next occurrence of the word and then select *Replace.* Choose the desired option.

6. Click on *Close.*

CUTTING AND PASTING

Sometimes it may be necessary to move a section of text from one location to another. This action is commonly referred to as *cutting and pasting.* There are several ways of accomplishing this task. Three methods will be highlighted.

METHOD 1

1. Block the text to be moved.

2. Click on the *Cut icon.* ⟶

3. Position the insertion point at the place where the text is to be inserted.

4. Click on the *Paste icon.* ⟶

METHOD 2

1. Block the text to be moved.

2. Position the pointer on the blocked text. (Ensure that the pointer has the shape of an arrow).

3. Depress the left mouse button and drag the text to its new position.

METHOD 3

1. Block the text to be moved.

2. Position the pointer on the blocked text. (Ensure that the pointer has the shape of an arrow).

3. Click on the right mouse button. A pull down listing appears.

4. Select *Cut* (using left mouse button).

5. Now position the insertion point at the place where the text is to be inserted.

6. Click on the right mouse button. A pull down listing appears.

7. Click on *Paste* (using left mouse button).

TRY IT!

Type the following sentences one under the other:

Today is Sunday.

Tomorrow is Monday.

Yesterday was Saturday.

After typing **Saturday**, press <ENTER>

1. **Cut** the sentence **Today is Sunday**.

2. **Paste it** after **Yesterday was Saturday**.

Continue practising cutting and pasting. (Do not close this file. You will be using it very soon).

COPYING AND PASTING

Instead of <u>moving</u> text to a new location, sometimes you may want to copy text.

To copy text:-

METHOD 1

    1. Block the text to be copied.

    2. Click on the **_Copy_** icon.   ⟶

    3. Position the insertion point where you desire the copy to be placed.

    4. Click on the **_Paste_** icon.   ⟶

METHOD 2

    1. Block the text to be copied.

    2. Position the mouse pointer on the blocked text. (It must be an arrow).

    3. Keep the **<CTRL>** key depressed and click and drag the text to the other location.

METHOD 3

    1. Block the text to be copied.

    2. Position the mouse pointer on the blocked text.(It must be an arrow).

    3. Click on the right mouse button. (A pull down menu appears).

    4. Select **_Copy_** (using left mouse button).

    5. Position the insertion point where you want the copy to be placed.

    6. Click on the right mouse button.

    7. Select **_Paste_** (using left mouse button).

In reference to the sentences recently typed (i.e. **Today is Sunday** etc.) make the following changes.

1. Copy the sentence, **Tomorrow is Monday.**

2. Position the copy before the words **Today is Sunday**.

Continue practising copying and pasting.

COLLECT AND PASTE

When Microsoft Word cuts or copies text, for example, it stores it in something called a *clipboard.* When you paste, you copy an item from the clipboard into your document.

Microsoft Word 2000 has a feature that allows you to cut or copy a number of items (text or graphics etc.), and paste them onto your document in any order.

To utilize this feature all you have to do is.

1. Cut/copy a number of items.

   As you do so the clipboard toolbar should appear.

   (If the clipboard toolbar does not appear, access it by clicking on the **View** menu. Select **Toolbars.** In the listing that appears, select **Clipboard.** The toolbar should now appear.)

   On the clipboard are icons that represent each item cut or copied. (Just point at an icon to get an indication of the object or text it represents.)

2. When you are ready to paste, simply click on the appropriate icon from the clipboard.

Microsoft Word can store up to twelve objects/items on the clipboard at any one time.

PRACTICE — EXERCISE 6 A

1. Type the following document and execute the instructions given below.

One day some strangers visited her home. She was very excited! You see the adults who came to visit her parents also had two handsome sons and a daughter who seemed to be around her age. Immediately she conjured up images of them all playing together around the lake. She hoped that they were interested in the vacant house a short distance from her home.

There was once a beautiful girl who lived in a beautiful house at the side of a beautiful lake. Despite her cheerful surroundings, she was very lonely. She had no brothers or sisters and her parents were very old.

2. **Cut** the first paragraph. (Notice you were not instructed to paste it).

3. **Copy** the second paargraph. (Notice you were not instructed to paste it).

4. **Paste** the 'cut' paragraph after the paragragh currently displayed.

5. **Paste** the 'copied' paragraph after the last paragraph currently displayed.

6. **Replace** all occurrences of the word **beautiful** with **gorgeous** without deleting the word **beautiful**.

7. Save the document as **Exercise 6 A.**

PRACTICE — EXERCISE 6 B

1. Type the following document and execute the instructions given below.

If you have a **GOOD SELF ESTEEM,** it means that you have accepted yourself as you are. You see, we all have faults but we must be able to accept ourselves with these faults. Every young person needs to have a **healthy feeling** about himself/herself. There may be some things about yourself that you do not like and that you will not be able to change, yet you **MUST ACCEPT YOURSELF**.

Improving Your Self Esteem.

2. **Cut** the third sentence in the passage and paste it at the beginning of the passage.

3. **Move** the heading at the bottom of the document and position it above the passage.

4. **Embolden, double-underline** and apply the **All caps** effect to the heading.

5. Change the font and font size of the heading to **Broadway, 16.**

6. Change the font and the font size of the passsage to **Tahoma, 11.**

7. Change the margins to **0.8".**

8. **Copy** the final sentence in the passage and position it immediately after the first sentence.

9. **Copy** the paragraph and paste it below the paragraph currently dislayed.

10. Insert a **Page break** after the first paragraph.

11. Change the line spacing to **1.5 lines.**

12. There are now two pages, number them using the numbering format:- **a,b,c.**

13. Save the document as **Excercise 6 B**.

PRACTICE — EXERCISE 6 C

1. Type the following document and execute the instructions given below.

Operating System

An **operating system** is a collection of processor programs (instruction) which controls and coordinates the overall operations of the processor. It provides temporary _storage_ for programs.

Random Access Memory

RAM is the _electronic memory_ that the processor uses to store information until it is desired or stored.

_____

2. Replace all occurrences of the word **processor** with **computer.**

3. Insert the following header at the top right-hand corner:- **Basic notes on computers.**

4. Cut the final sentence of the first paragraph and paste it after the first sentence below the heading **Random Access Memory.**

5. Copy the heading **Random Access Memory** and the passage associated with it and paste it at the top of the document.

6. Copy the heading **Operating System** and the passage associated with it and paste it at the end of the document.

7. Appropriately divide your document into two parts. Set the margins for one part to **0.8"** all around and the other to **1"** all around.

8. Save the document as **Exercise 6 C.**

THE SPELL CHECK A B C

You may have noticed that sometimes while you are typing, some text may be underlined by a wavy red line, and others, by a wavy green line. The wavy red line indicates that a possible spelling error exists and the wavy green line indicates that a possible grammatical error exists.

Now you will learn how to check the spelling in a document.

Checking the spelling in your document is easy.

Either click on the ***Spelling and Grammar*** icon,

OR Select ***Tools*** on the menu bar and then select ***Spelling and Grammar.***

The ***Spelling and Grammar*** dialogue box appears and Microsoft Word then checks the spelling and grammar for you.

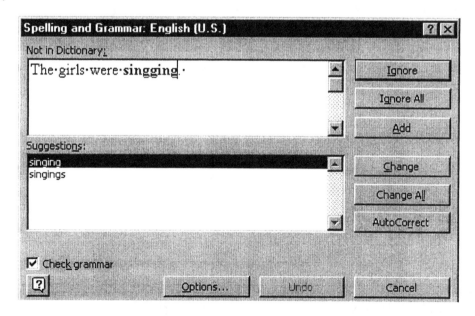

POINTS TO NOTE

Microsoft Word has its own dictionary of words. Anytime you type a word it checks its dictionary to see whether that word occurs in its dictionary. If the word is not in its dictionary, that word is highlighted as a word that is possibly incorrectly spelt and is displayed in the text box beneath **_Not In Dictionary._** Incorrectly spelt words are highlighted in red lettering and words for which grammatical errors have been identified, are displayed in green lettering.

Four basic actions are performed when using the Spell Check:

1. **Change**   You select this button when you want to change the spelling of the word highlighted, to a suggestion in the text box underneath **_Suggestions._**

2. **Ignore**   You select this button when a word displayed is actually correctly spelt.

3. **Delete**   This button is selected when a word has been repeated twice in succession and you wish to delete one occurrence.

4. **Add**   You select this button when you wish to add a word to the computer's dictionary.

You can correct inaccurate spelling by: -

1. Selecting the correct spelling from the list of suggestions and then clicking on the **_Change_** command button.

2. Typing the correct spelling directly, in the text box below **_Not in Dictionary,_** and then clicking on the **_Change_** command button.

OR

3. Clicking twice in the document itself and making the correction there. (Click on the **_Resumé_** button in the **_Spelling and Grammar_** dialogue box to resume the spell check.)

*If the checkmark next to **Check Grammar** has not been deactivated then both Spelling and Grammar will be checked simultaneously. (The procedure for checking grammar is quite similar to that for checking spelling.)*

*If you do not wish to check the grammar in the document, deactivate the checkmark next to the option to **Check Grammar** (in the **Spelling and Grammar** dialogue box).*

 ***Things to remember:-***

- Occasionally words are displayed which are actually correctly spelt. They are displayed because the computer is not familiar with them. These should be ***Ignored***.

- If a word is repeated twice in succession (e.g. a a boy), one of the repeated words is highlighted as an error. This should be ***Deleted***.

- If a word has been typed ***directly after*** a punctuation mark for example, a full stop with no space between (e.g. game.The),this is identified as an error. Simply insert a space between the punctuation mark and the word and select ***Change***.

TRY IT!

TYPE: **The brds is flying in the sky.They are vry beuteful.**

- Place your insertion point at the beginning of the sentence and activate the **SpellCheck**. When you are finished, your sentence should look like this:

    The birds are flying in the sky. They are very beautiful.

Microsoft Word 2000 also provides you with a ***Thesaurus*** that can be used to find the synonyms of words within your document.

To use the Thesaurus, simply: -

1. Block the text for which the synonym is desired.

2. Select the _**Tools**_ menu.

3. Select _**Language.**_

4. Select _**Thesaurus.**_ (A dialogue box appears.) Within this box you are given the option of replacing the blocked word with any of the synonyms identified. (Bear in mind that synonyms are not always found.) To select a synonym, click on it.

5. Click on either the **_Replace_** or **_Cancel_** button,

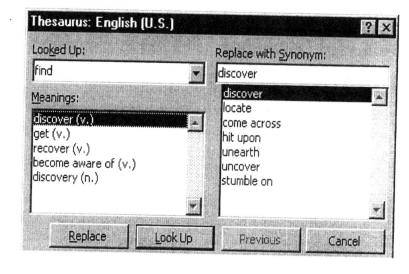

TRY IT!

Type the following exactly as it appears (bad spelling and all!).

Aljerone and Suzette as pling in the parke whn a bigg blck truk apered from nowhere, carring prisoners.The children were scarred.

1. **Perform a Spell Check** on the passage.
   After the Spell Check your two sentences should look like this. -

Aljerone and Suzette were playing in the park when a big black truck appeared from nowhere, carrying prisoners. The children were scared.

2. Find appropriate **synonyms** for the words **scared** and **big.**

From now on, practise performing a **_Spell Check_** on all your documents.

TEST PREPARATION

In preparation for **Self Test 3**, teachers are required to type the passage below in the same format as it appears and save the file as **Test 3**. Then copy the file to the students' diskettes.

---

ergocentrics is the *"science of work"*. It is the science of <u>designing or arranging machines</u> and objects that people use in the work environment, in a manner that takes into consideration peoples' capabilities and limitations.

The object of the field of ergocentrics is to improve work performances and hence achieve greater productivity by removing sources of <u>muscular stress and general fatigue</u>. The machines and objects that people use in the work environment are not only designed to be <u>user friendly</u>, but are arranged in the workplace to ease stress and fatigue.

Ergonomics

SELF TEST 3

<u>SECTION A</u>

FOLLOW THE INSTRUCTIONS GIVEN BELOW.

a) Open the file on your diskette called **Test 3**.

b) Some words in the passage were underlined for emphasis. Remove the underline and italicize those words.   **(2 Marks)**

c) **Move** the main heading **Ergonomics** from the bottom of the document and position it at the top of your document.   **(2 Marks)**

d) **Copy** the second paragraph and paste it so that it appears as the first paragraph.   **(2 Marks)**

e) **Change** the margins of the document to **1.2"** on the left and right margins and **1.4"** on the top and bottom margins.   **(1 Mark)**

f) Centre and double-underline the main heading at the top of the document.

Change the font to Garamond and the font size to 16. Display the heading in the Title case format. **(4 Marks)**

g) Justify the passage. **(1 Mark)**

h) Replace all occurrences of the word **ergocentrics** with **ergonomics**. **(2 Marks)**

i) Change the page orientation of the document to **landscape**. **(1 Mark)**

j) Apply Small caps to all occurrences of the word **ergonomics**. **(2 Marks)**

k) Insert a header at the **top right-hand corner** of the page and type your **name and class**. **(3 Marks)**

1) Save the document as **Test 3 A** and close it.

[Sub Total - 20]

SECTION B

a) Open the file **Test 3 A.**

b) Change the **margins** to **1.3"** at the top and bottom margins and **2.8"** at the right and left margins. **(2 Marks)**

c) Change the line spacing to **double line spacing.** **(1 Mark)**

d) Insert **footer** at the left-hand corner of the document and type the name of your school. **(3 Marks)**

e) Insert **a Page break** at the end of each paragraph so that each paragraph begins on a new page. **(3 Marks)**

f) Number each page. Numbers must appear at the bottom right-hand corner of each page. **(1 Mark)**

g) Save the file as **Test 3 B**.

[Sub Total - 10]

[Total - 30]

CHAPTER 7

TABLES

At the end of this chapter you should be able to:-

- Create a table.
- Format a table using Table Auto Format.
- Format text within a table.
- Move and resize a table.
- Change table alignment.
- Insert rows and columns within a table.
- Delete rows and columns from a table.
- Delete a table.
- Increase /decrease the width/height of a column/row.
- Change text alignment.
- Change text orientation.
- Sort the data in a table.

CREATING TABLES

PARTS OF A TABLE

Before you insert a table you must know the parts of a table.
A table has cells, columns and rows. The following diagram below illustrates this.

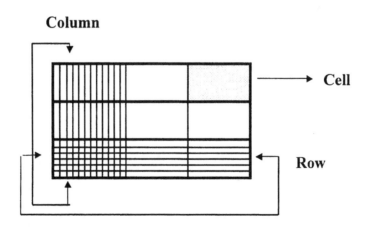

To insert a table in your document:-

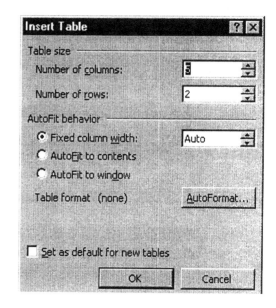

1. Ensure that the insertion point is at the place where the table is to be inserted.

2. Select the ***Table*** menu.

3. Select the ***Insert*** command and then ***Table*** from the sub-listing that appears (The ***Insert Table*** dialogue box is displayed).

4. In the dialogue box indicate the number of columns and rows the table should have.

Your table can be inserted with an attractive format.
To see the various formats available:-

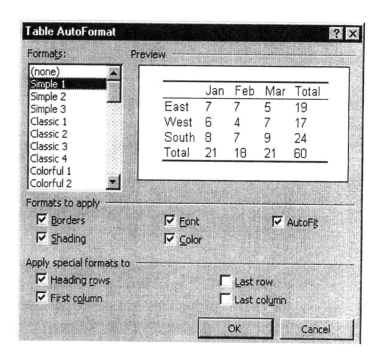

1. Click on the ***Auto Format*** button. Another dialogue box appears.

2. Click on the various formats on the left (e.g. ***Simple 2***), and observe the appearance of the table in the preview area. (Ignore the content of the table. Focus on its appearance).

3. Click on the format preferred and click on ***OK***. (The ***Insert Table*** dialogue box appears again).

4. Click on ***OK***.

You now have a table in your document with the same format as the one previously selected.

If you wish to change the format of your table afterwards:-

1. Position the insertion point in the table.

2. Select the *Table* menu.

3. Select *Table AutoFormat*. (The *Table AutoFormat* dialogue box appears). If you did not place your insertion point within the table the *Table AutoFormat* option would not be visible.

   (**N.B.** Whenever the *AutoFit* check box is activated, it means that the table will be reduced to a default size. To maintain the size of your table, deactivate the *AutoFit* check box.)

4. In the dialogue box, select the format preferred.

5. Click on *OK*.

INSERTING TEXT WITHIN TABLES

Do this little exercise. You are about to add text to the table. Click within any cell and type an arbitrary word. Having done that, press <ENTER>. What happened? You should have noticed that the row increased in height. That is lesson number one. If you press <ENTER> within a cell it simply makes the row taller. It does not move the insertion point to the cell below.

NOTE

• To move your insertion point to the cell below, you need to use the arrow key that points downward (or you can click on the cell).

• To move your insertion point to the cell on the right, you can press <TAB> or press the arrow key that points to the right.

BLOCKING CELLS, COLUMNS AND ROWS

You can block the text within a table in the same manner that you block normally. However, there are other techniques that might be useful to know. Below are two other methods for blocking cells, columns and rows.

METHOD 1

The diagram below illustrates where the mouse pointer should be positioned to block the areas identified.

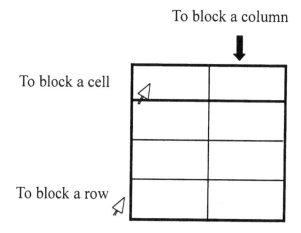

To block a column, the mouse pointer must change to a black arrow. To block a row and a cell the mouse pointer should have the shape of an outlined arrow.

To block a cell, column or row:-

1. Position the pointer at the appropriate position and click.

METHOD 2

1. Place the insertion point in the cell, row or column you want to block.

2. Click on the *Table* menu.

3. Click on *Select*.

4. Click on either cell, row or column from the sub-listing that appears (You can block the entire table by clicking on **Table**).

With a cell, row or column blocked you can easily format the text within a table.

MOVING A TABLE - THE TABLE MOVE HANDLE

If you position your pointer on your table you should see the ***table move handle*** appear at the top left corner.

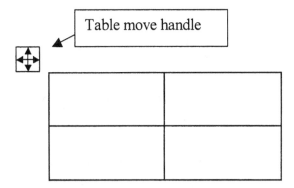

If you position your pointer on this handle and click and drag, you can move the table in any direction.

Try moving your table with the table move handle.

CHANGING THE SIZE OF A TABLE - THE TABLE RESIZE HANDLE

If you position your pointer on the table once more, you would notice the ***table resize handle*** at the bottom right corner. Position your pointer over this handle and your pointer takes the shape of a double headed arrow. If you were to click and drag now, the table would become bigger, but the number of columns and rows would not change.

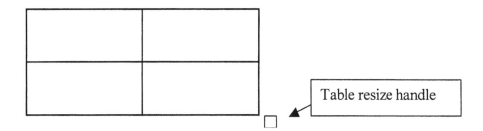

Try resizing your table with the table resize handle.

TABLE PROPERTIES

Table Properties is a very useful facility in Microsoft Word2000 as it allows you to vary the location of your table and also to control the wrapping of text about your table. (When text is wrapped around your table, it means that text is typed around your table.)

To access Table Properties:-

1. Place insertion point within the table.

2. Click on the *Table* menu.

3. Select *Table Properties*. (*Table Properties* dialogue box is displayed).

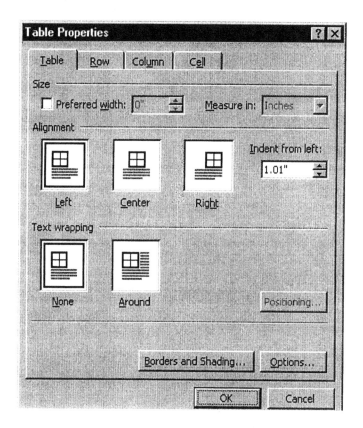

4. Click on the *Table* tab at the top of the box.

5. Under *Alignment*, select the alignment you want by clicking on the appropriate box.

6. Under *Text Wrapping* decide whether or not you want text about your table.

7. Click on *OK*.

1. Insert a table in your document similar in format to the one below. (The names of the countries are in **Small Caps**). Use the suggested font and font size.

Font - **Arial**   Font size - **14**

Country	Agriculture	Industry	Services
ARGENTINA	13	34	53
BRAZIL	31	27	42
CHILE	17	25	58
MEXICO	37	29	35
PERU	40	18	42

2. Insert the heading — **Structure of the Labour Force, 1980** — above the table.

3. Change the alignment of the table on the page, to centre.

4. Centre all the values in the table.

5. Save the file as **Exercise 7 A**.

PRACTICE — EXERCISE 7 B

1. Insert a table in your document and type in the given information. Use the suggested font and font size.

Font - **Garamond**   Font size - **14**

Action	Purpose	Procedure
Clicking	Used to select something.	Briefly depress the left button.
Double-Clicking	Used to start programmes.	Press the left button twice, quickly!
Dragging	Used to highlight areas on the screen or to move objects around on the screen.	Keep the left button depressed while you slide the mouse in the desired direction. Now release it.

2. Insert heading — **Using a Mouse** — above the table.

3. **Capitalize** the column headings.

4. **Italicize** all the text within the table (including the headings).

5. Save the file as **Exercise 7 B**.

INSERTING COLUMNS/ROWS

To insert additional columns within a table:-

1. Place the insertion point in the column.

2. Select the *Table* menu.

3. Select *Insert*. Another listing appears.

To explain the significance of the options displayed, consider this example.

This is a table with a column blocked.

46	
39	

The two tables below depict the **result** when each of the following options is selected.

(Remember you want to insert a column).

<table>
<tr><th colspan="2">OPTION A
Columns to the Left</th></tr>
</table>

OPTION A
Columns to the Left

	46	
	39	

OPTION B
Columns to the Right

46		
39		

This option inserts a column
to the **left** of the column blocked.

This option inserts a column
to the **right** of the column blocked.

4. Now choose whether you want to insert your column to the left or to the right, and click on the respective option.

If you want to insert a row, a similar procedure must be followed. Position the insertion point in a row, click on the *Table* menu, select *Insert*, and decide whether you want to insert the row above or below the blocked row.

DELETING COLUMNS/ROWS

Deleting a cell, column or row is an even simpler process than that highlighted above. Position the insertion point in the cell, column or row. Click on the *Table* menu. Select *Delete* and choose the appropriate option from the listing that appears.

CHANGING COLUMN WIDTH AND ROW HEIGHT

Sometimes you may wish to adjust the width of the columns of your table.

To change the width of a column:-

1. Position the **insertion point** in the table.

2. Position the mouse pointer **ON** the ***column marker*** which appears on the horizonal ruler.

3. When your mouse pointer changes to a double-headed arrow (↔) ,click and drag in the desired direction (to the left or right).

To change the height of a row:-

1. Position the **insertion point** in the table.

2. Position the mouse pointer on the ***row marker*** on the vertical ruler.

3. When it changes to a double-headed arrow (↔), click and drag in the desired direction (up or down).

Remember you can only drag in the directions indicated on the double-headed arrows.

PRACTICE — EXERCISE 7 C

1. Produce a duplicate of the table below, using the suggested font and font size.

Font - **Geometr 231 Lt Bt.**   Font size - **14**

Information to be typed .... ────────────────────────────────

Please be advised that taxi fares have been increased. The new fares are indicated below.

Route	Adults
Curepe to Tacarigua	$5.00
Arima to D'Abadie	$4.00
St. Joseph to St. Augustine	$3.00
Maraval to Laventile	$9.00

End of typing ────────────────────────────────

1. Insert the main heading **New Taxi Fares** immediately above the table.

2. **Bold, capitalize, centre** and **double-underline** the main heading.

3. Change the font size of the main heading to 22.

4. **Embolden** and apply the **Small caps** effect to the column headings.

5. Change the format of the table to **Classic 2**.

6. Insert a row immediately above **Arima to D'Abadie** and insert the following information:-

   Port of Spain to San Fernando $8.00

7. Insert a column before **Adults** and enter the following information:

Children under twelve
$4.50
$3.00
$2.00
$1.50
$5.00

8. Centre all the values in the table.

9. Embolden and italicize the contents of the column **Route**.

10. Save the document as **Exercise 7 C**.

11. Delete the column whose column heading is — **Adults**.

12. Delete the row with the route — **Arima to D'Abadie**.

13. Right-align the values in the table.

14. Centre the table on the page.

15. Change the format of your table to **List 7**.

16. Save the file as **Exercise 7 C 1**.

PRACTICE — EXERCISE 7 D

1. Produce a duplicate of the table below and execute the instructions that follow. Use the suggested font and font size.

Font - Geometr231 Lt Bt.   Font - 14

INFOFLIGHT SOFTWARE LTD. MONTHLY SALES

SOFTWARE	KINGSTON	MANDEVILLE	MO-BAY	OCHO RIOS
Word Processing	$220,000	$75,000	$135,000	$70,000
Database	$195,000	$60,000	$92,000	$50,000
Spreadsheets	$110,000	$30,000	$70,000	$40,000

2. Insert a row immediately under the row heading **"Database"** and insert the following information:-

Graphics	$180,000	$90,000	$80,000

3. Delete the column whose column heading is — **Ocho Rios.**

4. Insert a column at an appropriate point within the table
   and include the following information:

TOTAL
$430,000
$252,000
$210,000
$300,000

5. **Centre** the table on the page.

6. Change the format of the table **List 4**.

7. Save the document as **Exercise 7 D**.

PRACTICE — EXERCISE 7 E

Look carefully at the given information and carry out the following instructions.

The following represents the percentages that some students received in two math tests given.

George Ennis	70	75
Evan Muir	65	73
Faith Wayne	60	78
Steven Watt	92	96
Sharon Tomlinson	83	79
Erica Nunes	52	68
Henry Richards	76	80

1. After identifying appropriate headings for each column, insert the headings as well as the data on page 109, in a table.

2. Format the table using the **Columns 3** format.

3. **Italicize** all the students' names and **embolden** the column headings.

4. Change the font of the text in the table to **Tahoma** and **centre** it.

5. **Centre** all the marks in their columns.

6. The entry for **Eric Nunes** was incorrectly entered. **Remove his entire record** from the table.

7. **Insert** a new column between the column with the students' names and the column with the first set of recorded marks. In the new column, enter the heading **ID Number** and for each student enter an arbitrary ID number.

8. Save the document as **Table 4**.

A FEW USEFUL TIPS

Sometimes you may want to create a table with numerous rows. These rows may span more than one page. When you print, you will want the column headings of your table to print on each page without you having to retype the headings. With Microsoft Word 2000, this is a simple task.

All you have to do is:-

1. Block the column headings that should appear on each page. (This should include the first row of the table).

2. Click on the *Table* menu.

3. Select *Heading Rows Repeat*.

SORTING

To sort the entries in your table all you have to do is:-

1. Block the table (You can exclude the column headings).

2. Click on the *Table* menu.

3. Select **Sort**.

4. In the dialogue box that appears, choose the column that has the data to be sorted.

   (The first column to the left of the spreadsheet is **Column 1**).

5. Choose the order (whether ascending or descending order).

6. If you have blocked the header row (which is your column heading), activate **My List has Header row**, otherwise activate **My List has no header row**).

7. Click on **OK**.

CHANGING TEXT ORIENTATION

In a table, you can display text horizontally or vertically (as indicated in the example below).

Example:-

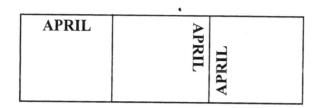

To make this adjustment:-

1.   Block the text in the table.

2.   Click on the **Format** menu.

3.   Select **Text Direction**. A dialogue box appears.

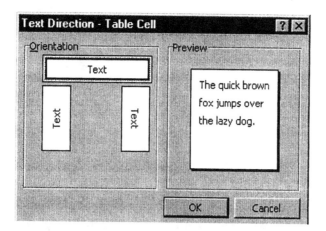

4. Choose the **Orientation** desired by clicking on the appropriate box.

5. Click on **OK**.

CHANGING TEXT ALIGNMENT

You can also control the alignment of the text in your table as the example below illustrates.

Example:-

APRIL		
	APRIL	
		APRIL

(Before doing this exercise you may need to increase the height of the rows in your table.)

To change text alignment:-

1. Block the cell.

2. Click on the **Table** Menu.

3. Select **Table Properties**.

4. Click on the **Cell** tab at the top of the dialogue box.

5. Choose the alignment desired by clicking on the appropriate box.

6. Click on **OK**.

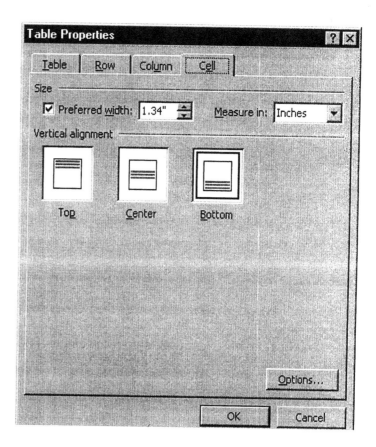

1. Type the following in the same format as it appears.

NAME	TEST 1	TEST 2
James, Louise	46	45
Thomas, Carla	39	38
Simpson, Terry	90	79
Dobson, Arlene	79	89
Adams, Brent	89	78
Booth, Michael	57	87

2. Sort the names of the students according to alphabetical order, ensuring that each record remains accurate. (i.e. Carla got 39 in Test 1. After sorting, her marks should not change).

3. Change the format of the table to **List 8**.

4. Save it as **Exercise 7 F**.

CHAPTER 8

PICTURES AND AUTOSHAPES

At the end of this chapter you should be able to:-

- Insert pictures.
- Move and change the size of pictures.
- Format pictures.
- Insert Autoshapes.
- Move and change the size of AutoShapes.
- Add fill colour to AutoShapes.
- Add line colour to AutoShapes.

INSERTING PICTURES

This is the time most students like you have been waiting for. Many people enjoy using pictures to enhance their documents. Some may use a picture to make the cover page of an assignment more attractive. Others may use it to make the message on a sign more effective. Now you will learn how to insert pictures in your document.

To insert pictures in your document:-

1. Position the insertion point at the location where the picture is to be inserted.

2. Select the **_Insert_** menu.

3. Select **_Picture_**.

4. Select the sub-menu **_Clip Art_**. A dialogue box appears.

5. In the dialogue box, you will notice that the pictures have been divided into categories. Each category is represented by a picture. (e.g. Academic, Animals etc.). Notice there is a vertical scroll bar. This means you can scroll to see other categories. Look for the category in which you think your picture could be found. Click on the ***category***.

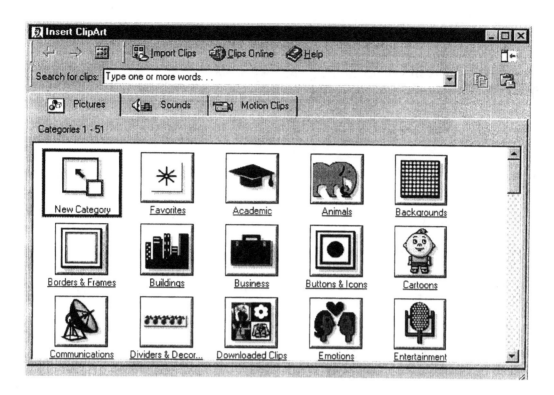

(Microsoft Word2000 also allows you to type in a word or words describing the kind of picture you desire. Instead of clicking on a category, you can click in the text box area that says *Type one or more words*. After typing the words press <ENTER>. The computer will search for the pictures).

6. Now you should see several pictures that are in the category you selected. If you do not like any of these pictures, use the vertical scroll bar to go to the last picture. At this point, if you see the words *Keep Looking*, then there are other pictures in the category, that are not yet displayed. Click on *Keep Looking* to see other pictures in the category. (If *Keep Looking* is not visible, then the computer can locate no other pictures represented by the word typed.)

(At the top left of the dialogue box, you should see an arrow pointing to the left and another to the right. If at any time you wish to go back to pictures seen previously, click on the arrow that points to the left. If you keep clicking on that button, you will eventually return to the display of all the categories.)

7. When you have eventually found the picture you like, *click* on it. A call out appears with buttons on it. As you point at each button, a word appears indicating the function of that particular button. The first button on the call out usually is the *Insert clip* button. **Click** on it and the picture selected will be inserted in the document.

(If the *Insert Clip Art* dialogue box is still displayed, you have the option to close it or minimize it so that you can continue working in your document.)

Now try inserting a picture in your document.

CHANGING THE SIZE OF A PICTURE

When you insert a picture in your document, you may decide that it is either too large or too small. So now you must learn how to change the size of a picture.

To change the size of a picture:-

1. Click in the immediate area around the picture to activate it. A border with small boxes/ handles should appear about the picture.

2. Position the mouse pointer on any of the small black handles that appear along the border. The pointer should take the shape of a double-headed arrow (↕ ⟷ ↗ ↘)

3. Click and drag to change the size of the picture. (You must drag in any one of the directions in which the arrow is pointing).

4. Click outside the immediate area around the picture to deactivate it.

Try to change the size of the picture you had inserted previously.

Before you can make any change to a picture, it must be activated. When a picture is activated the handles appear around it. To activate a picture simply click on it. To deactivate it, click anywhere outside the picture.

MOVING A PICTURE

To reposition or move a picture:-

1. Activate the picture.

2. Click on any of the alignment buttons (i.e. left, right or centre).

If you want to move the picture just a little:-

1. Position the **insertion point** to the left of the picture.

2. Press the **<TAB>** key or the spacebar.

Now move your picture to the centre and to the right.

FORMATTING A PICTURE

When you have inserted a picture in your document, you cannot insert text anywhere along the side of the picture. You can only type above and below the picture. Insert a picture and try to type to the side of it. Nothing works better or is more understood that trying it out yourself. Seeing is believing!

In order to position the text at the side of the picture you must format the picture, thereby allowing text to wrap around the picture.

To format a picture:-

1. Activate the picture.

2. Click on the *Format* menu.

3. Select *Picture*. A dialogue box appears.

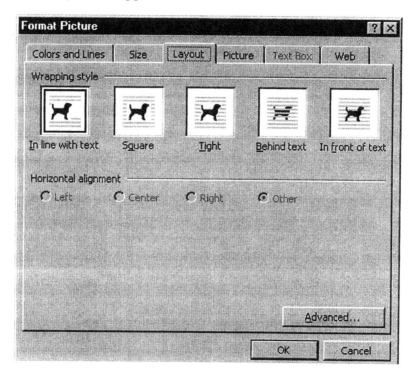

4. Select the *Layout* tab towards the top of the dialogue box. Different wrapping styles should be displayed.

5. Here you are given several options as to how the text could be positioned in relation to the picture. (e.g. The *Tight* style wraps text tightly around the picture). Select one of the wrapping styles by clicking on its diagrammatic representation. Click on *OK*.

After you have formatted a picture, the procedure for moving it changes.

To move a picture after you have formatted it:-

1. Click on it (to activate it).

2. Position your pointer anywhere within the picture. (NOT ON THE HANDLES).

3. Click and drag to the desired position.

You can also move a picture by pressing on the keyboard.

To delete a picture, click on it and press <DELETE>.

Type the following passage below in the same format as it appears. Use the suggestions in the box.

Font — Arial	*Text position* — 0.9"
Font size of passage — 12	*Bullet position* — 0.6"
Font size of words at end — 26	

<u>KEY POINTS FOR SMALL BUSINESSES</u>

If your business has been built on a <u>SOLID FOUNDATION</u> and you have maintained a careful record of business accounts, ***disasters should not occur***. The following are some of the reasons why businesses collapse.

- Lack of expertise

- Poor management

- Inadequate resources.

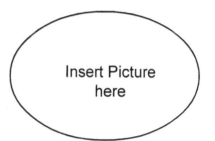

NEVER IGNORE CASH FLOW PROBLEMS OR A DROP IN BUSINESS.

SUCCESS CAN BE YOURS

Save the file as **Exercise 8 A**.

INSERTING AUTOSHAPES

In addition to pictures, you can insert interesting shapes in your document. Before attempting to draw, ensure that the **Drawing toolbar** is displayed. The drawing toolbar is a toolbar usually located towards the bottom of your monitor. (The first button on the toolbar is the **Dr̲aw** button). If the drawing toolbar is not displayed, click on the **Drawing button** on the standard toolbar.

Now you will learn to insert a variety of shapes.

To draw an AutoShape:-

1. Click on the **A̲utoShapes** button on the Drawing toolbar. A listing appears.

2. All the shapes have been divided into categories. Point at each category (e.g. Lines, Basic Shapes etc.) to see the various shapes.

    To choose a shape, click on it.

3. After clicking on it, position your pointer within your document and you should notice that it now has the shape of a cross. Click and drag to draw the shape.

Notice that to the right of the **A̲utoShapes** button on the Drawing toolbar, are the *line, arrow, rectangle* and *oval* buttons. (Each is represented by a button with their respective shapes displayed).

Instead of clicking on AutoShapes, you can also draw these shapes by:-

1. Clicking on the appropriate button on the Drawing toolbar.

2. Clicking and dragging within the document window to insert the shape.

If you desire to draw a square:-

1. Click on the button that represents a rectangle.

2. Press the **<SHIFT>** key while dragging to insert a square.

If you desire to draw a circle:-

1. Click on the button that represents an oval.

2. Press the **<SHIFT>** key while dragging to insert a circle.

MOVING AN AUTOSHAPE

To move an AutoShape:-

1. Activate it.

2. Use the arrow keys to move it in the desired direction or position the pointer on it and click and drag.

NOTE

- *To delete an AutoShape*, activate it and press the **<DELETE>** key.

- The procedure for changing the size of an AutoShape is similar to that used to change the size of a picture.

- Before attempting to make any modification to an AutoShape remember to activate it first.

INTRODUCING THE FILL COLOUR BUTTON

Insert a picture in a document (any picture) and draw a rectangle about your picture as indicated below.

**Insert picture
here**

If your picture disappeared, do not panic! That is supposed to happen. Your picture disappeared because when the rectangle was inserted, it was automatically inserted with a *white* fill colour. *Fill colour* is the colour that fills the shape.

To remove the fill colour:-

1. Activate the rectangle.

2. Pass your pointer slowly along the Drawing toolbar. As you do so you will notice that words pop up indicating the function of each particular button. You need to find the *Fill Colour* button, so pass your pointer along the Drawing toolbar until you see the words *Fill Colour*.

Click on the small arrow to the **immediate** right of that button. A set of colours should appear.

3. At the top you should see a button marked | No Fill | Click on it.

Now you should see your picture.

From this exercise you should realize that you can use a similar procedure to add a colour to a shape. Instead of selecting *No Fill*, you can select a colour.

- To change the colour of the line outlining the shape, click on the arrow to the immediate right of the *Line Colour* button and select the colour desired. (The *Line Colour* button is usually next to the *Fill Colour* button on the Drawing toolbar).

PRACTICE — EXERCISE 8 B

Type the following passage in the same format as it appears, using the suggestions in the box below.

Font/font size of heading - Impact, 18

Font /font size of passage - Courier New, 12

Table Format - Columns 5

Librarian Assistant Schedule

Please take note of the schedule for week the beginning August 30th 1999. All Librarian Assistants are reminded that they are expected to report for duty at least five minutes before the commencement of the work session.

NAME	DAY	TIME
Desmond Fisher	Monday	8:30 - 12:30p.m.
Mavis Hewitt	Monday	12:30 - 4:30 p.m.
Majorie Palmer	Tuesday	8:30 - 12:30p.m.
Tony Samuels	Tuesday	12:30 - 4:30 p.m.
Mavis Hewitt	Wednesday	8:30 - 12:30p.m.
Desmond Fisher	Wednesday	12:30 - 4:30 p.m.
Tony Samuels	Thursday	8:30 - 12:30p.m.
Majorie Palmer	Thursday	12:30 - 4:30 p.m.

Insert Picture Here.
(Draw the border also)

CHAPTER 9

MERGING DOCUMENTS

At the end of this chapter you should be able to: -

- Combine different documents.
- Use Mail Merge effectively.

COMBINING DIFFERENT DOCUMENTS

Very often you may have two separate documents that you want to combine to form one document. This presents no problem at all. This is very easily done.

To combine different documents:

1. Open the document into which you want the file to be inserted.

2. Place the insertion point at the position where you want the other document to be inserted.

3. Click on the ___Insert___ menu.

4. Select *Fi_l_e*. A dialogue box appears.

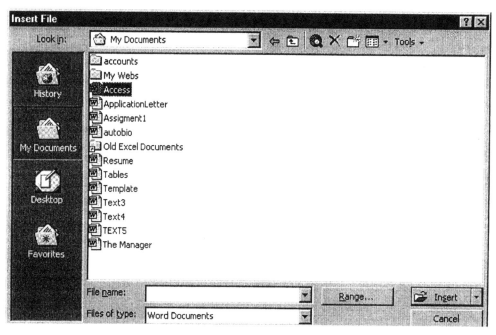

5. In the dialogue box which appears, select the drive and the name of the file you desire to insert.

6. Click on **OK**.

It may be wise to now save the merged document. If the two documents to be combined are on separate diskettes, it may be necessary to save at least one of the documents on the hard disk of the computer system being used, before performing the merge.

MAIL MERGE

Sometimes you may wish to send a copy of a similar document to several persons. Normally to do so you would need to first type the document, print it, then delete the person's name and address and type in another person's name and address, print it etc. If that document has to be sent to several persons, this task can become quite laborious. Microsoft Word provides an easier way to manage this activity. This is known as *Mail Merge*.

Mail Merge reduces the work involved when several copies of a similar document, addressed to different individuals, need to be produced.

To perform a mail merge, you need to:-

1. Create the *main document*. (The main document is the common information/letter that you wish to send to all individuals.)

2. Create the *data source*. (The data source would have the data that varies for each letter e.g. a person's name and address.)

3. Add the unique *fields* to the main document. (The fields are the areas where the unique information from the *data source* would be inserted.)

4. *Merge* the main document and the data document.

CREATING THE MAIN DOCUMENT

To create the main document simply:-

1. **Create** or **open** the document that
   is to be sent to various persons.
   (If the document is already
   opened start with step two).

2. **Click** the **Tools** menu.

3. **Choose** the **Mail Merge** option.
   (The **Mail Merge Helper** dialogue box is displayed).

4. **Click** the **Create** button to display
   the list of document types.

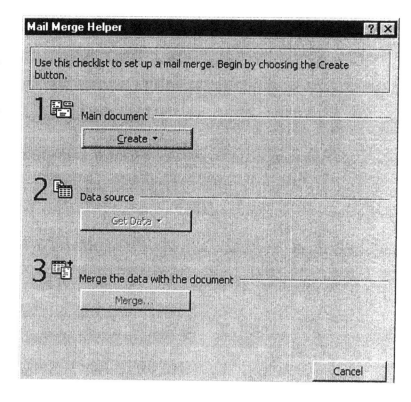

5. Choose **Form Letters**. A small dialogue box appears informing you that you can use the current
   document, or create a new document. Since the document is already open, select the **Active
   Windows** command button to convert this document into the main document.

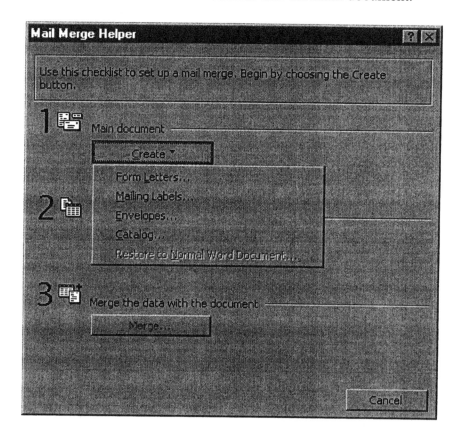

CREATING A DATA SOURCE

The *data source* is actually the information that is unique to each letter (e.g. a person's name and address). When creating the data source, you must first create the fields that accommodate this unique information. In other words, a person's first name could be stored in the *First Name* field and his/her address could be stored in the *Address* field.

To create the fields for the data source:-

1. In the *Mail Merge Helper* dialogue box, select *Get Data* (a drop-down list is displayed).

2. From the drop-down list, select *Create Data Source*. (The *Create Data Source* dialogue box appears.)

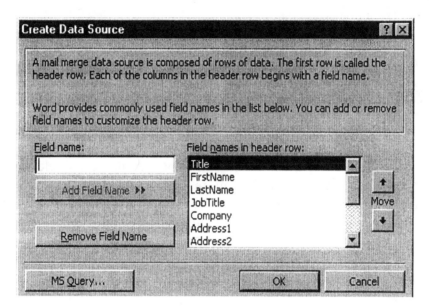

3. From the *Field names in the header row* list, choose a field you **DO NOT** want in your data source, and then select the *Remove Field Name* command button. This procedure is to be repeated to remove all fields you do not require in your data source.

4. If you wish to add a field which does not appear in the *Fields names in header row* list, type the name of the field in the *Field name* textbox, then click on the *Add Field Name* command button.

5. The *Field names in header row* list should now display all the fields that **YOU WANT** in your data source. Click on *OK* and the *Save Data Source* dialogue box is displayed. Save the data source the same way you would any other document.

6. After saving, a small dialogue box is displayed. Select the *Edit Data Source* command button to begin entering the data.

ENTERING DATA IN THE DATA SOURCE

You have added the fields. Now, you must enter the data that corresponds with these fields. So if you had entered *FirstName* and *LastName* as fields, now you will be entering the actual names of all the individuals to whom the letter must be sent. Upon selecting the *Edit Data Source* command button, the *Data Form* dialogue box is displayed. In this dialogue box, the fields that you had saved will appear and you will be required to enter the actual data into the corresponding text boxes.

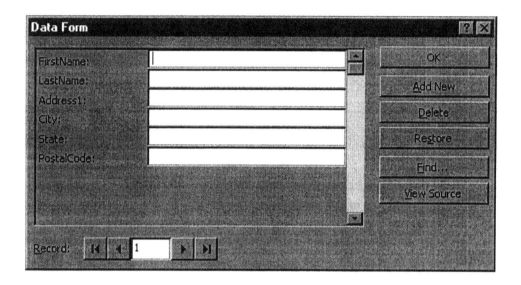

1. *Type* the appropriate data into each field. Upon entering data into each field, you now have what is referred to as a record. Notice that at the bottom left of the dialogue box, there are record selectors that, among other things, can give you an indication as to how many records have been created. Select the *Add New* command button to add the record to the data source file. Repeat this step to add all the necessary records to your data source file.

2. Click *OK*.

ADDING MERGE FIELDS

Having created the data source file that stores the data unique to each letter, you must now shift your attention once more to the main document. In the main document, you must now allocate areas where the information unique to each letter must be inserted. In other words, in your main document you must specify where the names will be inserted. To do so, you must create *merge fields*.

To add merge fields:-

1. In the main document, position the insertion point where you want to insert a merge field. (For example, position the insertion point where the recipient's name should go).

2. Click on the ***Insert Merge Field button*** on the ***Mail Merge toolbar*** to display a list of fields.

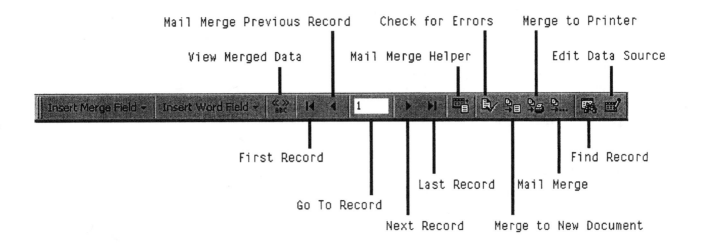

3. Select the merge field you want to insert.

4. Repeat steps 1 to 3 to insert merge fields at all the positions in the document where you want to use data from the data source.

5. Save the document.

STEP THREE

MERGING THE MAIN DOCUMENT AND THE DATA

You are now on the final leg — close to the finish line. Now you are ready to merge the main document and the data source file.

To merge the main document and the data source file:-

1. Select ***Mail Merge*** from the ***Tools*** menu.

2. Select the ***Merge*** button in the ***Merge the data with the document*** area. (The ***Merge*** dialogue box appears.)

3. From the ***Merge*** to drop down list box select ***new document*** or ***printer***.

4. In the ***Records to be merged*** area, indicate the range of records to be merged (i.e., ***All***.)

5. Click ***Merge*** to begin the merge.

MERGING TO A NEW DOCUMENT

When you select *New document* in the *Merge* dialogue box, the documents are merged to a file called *Form Letters 1*. In this file each letter is displayed with the name and address of the individual to whom it must be sent. All the letters are separated by a *Next Page Section Break* and can be saved and printed the same way you save and print other files.

MERGING TO A PRINTER

If you select *Merge to printer* in the *Merge* dialogue box, the *Print* dialogue box is displayed. Microsoft Word merges and prints a document(i.e. letter) for every data record in the data file. You select this option if you do not want to save the merged documents.

TESTING THE MERGE OPERATION

You can now test how well the two documents merged.

To test the merge operation you simply:-

1. Activate the main document, and click the *Check for errors* button on the *Mail Merge* toolbar. A *Checking and Reporting Errors* dialogue box is displayed with three options.

2. Select the first option *(Simulate the merge and report errors in a new document)*, and then click *OK*. If there are no mail errors, a message appears indicating no errors have been found. If errors are found, a dialogue box reports the nature of each error and one of the following options may be selected:-

    • Click the *Remove Field Name* button.
    • Replace an invalid field.
    • Click the *Cancel* button.

This all seems rather arduous. You may wonder if you are ever going to remember all these steps. There is only one way to ensure that you do remember. Just keep on practising for practice makes perfect.

PRACTICE — EXERCISE 9 A

You must send out application letters to five schools. You are given the letter (which is shown below), and the addresses of the schools. From the letter create the **main document** and use the addresses to form the **data source file**. Use the **Mail Merge** feature to **merge** both to form a **new document**. At the end of this exercise, you should have created a document that stores the five letters for the schools.

---

12 Queens St.,

Mandeville,

Jamaica.

The Principal,

<<School field>>

<< Address field>>

Dear Sir/Madam,

I am a recent graduate of the University of the West Indies where I obtained a Bachelor of Arts Degree in History (Upper Second Class Honours).

I wish to apply for a teaching position in your school, as I believe that my knowledge, experience and innate abilities will be a definite asset to you.

I will be available for an interview at your earliest convenience.

Yours sincerely,

_____

ALLISON MARKS

This letter has to be sent to five different schools. The addresses are indicated below:-

1) Mt. Helen High School, 4 Calex Ave., Portland, Jamaica.

2) Brown High School, 15 John Rd., Clarendon, Jamaica.

3) Trax High School, 23 Meadow St., Kingston 5, Jamaica.

4) Central High School, 2 Linton Drive, St. Mary, Jamaica.

5) Five Stones High School, 7 Shortwood Drive, Spanish Town, Jamaica.

PRACTICE — EXERCISE 9 B

There was a fight at your school involving five students. The principal has decided to suspend the five students pending a meeting with their parents. She therefore prepares a letter to inform the parents of the occurrence and her subsequent decision. You are given the letter (see page133), and the names and addresses of the parents. From the letter create the *main document* and use the addresses to form the *data source file*. Use the *Mail Merge* feature to merge both to form a *new document*. At the end of this exercise, you should have created a document that stores the five letters for the parents.

Use the suggestions given below:-

- Line spacing - 1.5 lines
- Font and font size of the name of the school — Times New Roman, 22

12 High St., St. Thomas, Jamaica, 973-1725

<<Title>><<ParentName field>>,

<<Address field>>

<<City>>

Dear Parent,

Your son **<<StudentName field>>** was involved in a fight today with some other students resulting in the damage of school property and minor injury to an innocent bystander.

I would appreciate a meeting with you at 8:30 a.m. in my office this coming Friday, so that we can discuss this matter, as the consequences of this act are quite serious. Please note that your son will not be permitted to attend classes until we have resolved this matter.

Yours sincerely,

_____

HELEN MARKS

Principal

The names and addresses of the five parents are listed below:-

Student's Name	Parent's Name	Address
1) John Brown	Mrs. Sandra Brown	4 Calex Ave., Portland, Jamaica.
2) Thomas Pane	Mr. Tony Pane	15 John Rd., Clarendon, Jamaica.
3) George James	Mr. Jonathan James	23 Meadow St., Kingston 5, Jamaica.
4) Henry Walton	Mr. Hilton Walton	2 Linton Drive, St. Mary, Jamaica.
5) Jerry Palmer	Mrs. Joyce Palmer	7 Shortwood Drive, Spanish Town, Jamaica.

EDITING AFTER MERGING

Sometimes after you have performed a mail merge, you realize that there are modifications to be made. For example, you may need to add new records to your data source file or you may simply have miss-spelt a word. In this section, you will explore the ways that adjustments can be made to your main document and data source file.

ADJUSTING YOUR MAIN DOCUMENT (FORM LETTER)

Adjustments to the main document can be made quite easily.

To adjust your main document:-

1. Open the main document.

2. Make your changes.

3. Save the changes made.

ADDING NEW RECORDS TO YOUR DATA SOURCE

Sometimes in your haste, you may forget to include a particular record. This poses no problem at all. There are many ways that new records can be added to your data source file.

METHOD 1

1. Open the main document.

2. Click on the **Edit Data Source** button on the Mail Merge Toolbar. (The **Data Form** dialogue box appears.)

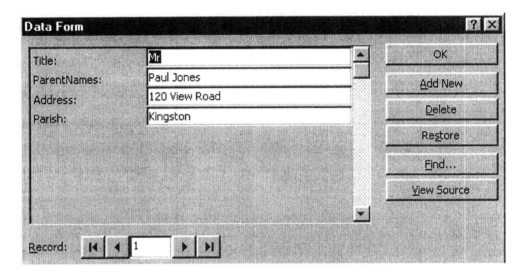

3. Select **Add New**.

4. Type in the new record.

5. Click on **OK**.

6. Click on the **Merge to New Document** button on the Mail Merge toolbar to re-merge the documents.

METHOD 2

1. Open the data source file.

2. Click on the **Add New Record** button on the database toolbar (A new row is inserted at the bottom of your table.)

3. Type in the new record.

4. Click on the *Save* button to save the changes you made.

5. Click on the *Mail Merge Main Document* button on the database toolbar (The main document appears). Note that this button will bring up the main document only if the main document is opened.

6. Click on the *Merge to New Document* button to re-merge the documents.

MODIFYING DATA RECORDS

To modify data records you simply:-

1. Open the main document.

2. Click on the *Edit Data Source* button. (The *Data Form* dialogue box appears).

3. Find the record you desire to edit and do so.

4. Click on *OK*.

5. Click on the *Merge to New Document* button to re-merge the documents.

OR

1. Open the data source file.

2. Directly edit the records stored in the table.

3. Save your changes.

4. Click on the *Mail Merge Main Document* button. (The main document appears.)

5. Click on the *Merge to New Document* button to re-merge the documents.

Whenever you re-merge the documents you must save the merged document.

MODIFYING FIELDS IN THE DATA SOURCE

To modify fields in the data source:-

1. Open the data source file.

2. Select the **Manage Fields** button on the database toolbar.

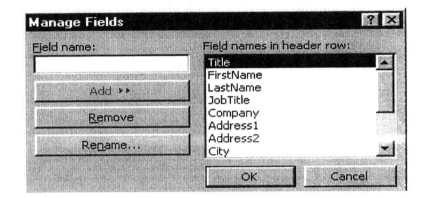

To add a field:-

3. Click in the ***Field name: box*** (The insertion point appears.)

4. In the ***Field name*** box type the name of the new field.

5. Select ***Add***.

To remove a field:-

1. Select the field you wish to remove.

2. Click on the ***Remove*** button.

To rename an existing field:-

1. Select the field that you wish to rename.

2. Click on the ***Rename*** button.

3. Type in the new name for the field in the ***New field*** name box.

4. Click on ***OK***.

After making all the required changes, save the data source file. Note, that if you add a new field to your data source file you must enter the data/record for that new field. To do so, follow methods 1 or 2 below the heading **ADDING NEW RECORD TO YOUR DATA SOURCE**.

As usual, you do have an alternative method of accomplishing the above task instead of following the steps outlined on page 137.

To add new records to your data source:-

1. Open the data source file.

2. Rename the field in the table directly.

3. Save your changes and ***close the file***.

If you want to insert a new field, simply insert a new column in the table and type in the new field and the data associated with the new field. Then save your changes and close the file.

After you have made modifications to your main document and/or your data source file, you need to re-merge your documents. The new merged document will reflect the changes you made.

RE-MERGING YOUR DOCUMENTS AFTER CHANGES HAVE BEEN MADE.

If you have made any modifications/additions to the field names in the data source file, you should ensure that the main document has been updated to reflect these changes. So, if you have renamed a field in the data source file, then the field name on the main document should also be adjusted, before you attempt to re-merge the document. For example, suppose you changed the field name from **Address** to **Residence**; before you re-merge the documents you need to delete the field name **Address** from the main document and insert the field name **Residence**. If you had inserted any new field you would also have to insert these new fields, at the appropriate place in the main document.

To re-merge the document:-

1. Open the main document.

2. Click on the ***Merge to New Document*** button.

You are given an application form (main document) and the data that should be placed in the application form (data source). You are required to use the *Mail Merge* feature to merge the main document given to produce three completely filled application forms.

APPLICATION FORM

Name <<LastName>>	<<FirstName>>	
	Surname **First name**	
Address: <<Address>>		**Tel:** <<Tel>>
Name of course: <<Course>>		

1. Have you ever done a computer course before (yes or no)? <<Answer>> _____

2. If you answered yes to the above question, list the courses that you have done, below.

   a) <<Course 1>> _____

   b) <<Course 2>> _____

   c) <<Course 3>> _____

3. Why do you want to do this course?

   <<Reasons>> _____

Thank You!

You will hear from us shortly!

FIELDS — NAMES AND DATA.

Last Name — Simpson

First Name — Sherry

Address — 5 John's Avenue, Spanish Town, Jamaica.

Tel — 984 -2647

Course — Microsoft Word

Answer — No

Course 1 —

Course 2 —

Course 3 —

Reason — I need to get a job and having computer skills would be an asset.

Last Name — Watkis

First Name — Jonathan

Address — 12 Point Terrace, Portmore, Jamaica.

Tel — 998-4362

Course — Microsoft Access

Answer — Yes

Course 1 — Microsoft Word

Course 2 — Microsoft Excel

Course 3 — Microsoft PowerPoint

Reason — I enjoy learning how to use software and I look forward to increasing my knowledge.

Last Name — Johnson

First Name — Larry

Address — 25 Park Avenue, Kingston 6, Jamaica.

Tel — 977-3542

Course — Microsoft Excel

Answer — Yes

Course 1 — Microsoft Word

Course 2 —

Course 3 —

Reason — As an accountant, I believe that this course will help me to work more efficiently.

TEST PREPARATION

In preparation for the exercise below you are required to open the file called **PROPOSAL** created in Chapter 4. Remove the sub-heading **Introduction** and the paragraph associated with it and position after the sub-heading **Ascetics** and the paragraph associated with it. Then save the document as **PROPOSAL 2**. Copy this file to the students' diskettes.

SELF TEST 4

SECTION A

Willsanie Construction company is submitting a proposal to the **Director**, *Public Works department,* the **Honourable Minister**, *The Ministry of Construction* and the **Permanent Secretary** in the *Ministry of Construction*, re the cleaning and repair of the gully beginning at Demshire Avenue and ending at Viewmount Crescent.

You are required to:-

a) Retrieve the file called **Proposal** from your diskette.

b) Set the top and bottom margins to **2 inches** and the left and right
margins to **0.8 inch**.   **(2 Marks)**

c) Change the page orientation of the proposal to **Landscape**.   **(1 Mark)**

d) Insert the title **Proposal to Clean and Repair Gully** at the top of the document.   **(1 Mark)**

e) **Embolden, double-underline** and **capitalize** the title.   **(1 Mark)**

f) Change the font and font size of the title to **Broadway** and **18** respectively.   **(1 Mark)**

g) Format the document into two newspaper style columns.   **(3 Marks)**

h) Move the heading **Introduction** and the passage associated with it
and position it above the sub-heading **Drainage**.   **(2 Marks)**

i) Replace all occurrences of the word **canal** with **gully**.   **(2 Marks)**

j) Insert a header at the top left hand corner of each page:-

       A Healthier Community   **(3 Marks)**

k) Below the heading *Equipment and Material* add the following *in a table*:-

Item	Unit Price	Total Price	
5 machetes	$120.00	$600.00	
6 hoes	$540.00	$3240.00	
3 hammers	$250.00	$750.00	**(3 Marks)**

l) Change the format of the table to *Columns 3*.   **(2 Marks)**

m) Between **machetes** and **hoes** add the following:-

    5 Push-brooms $160.00 $800.00   **(2 Marks)**

n) Insert a footer on each page using a small font and italics :-

        Labour cost will be based on the rates in effect at the time

        of work.   **(4 Marks)**

o) Insert bullets to itemize each repair work below the heading **Repair Work**. The Text position should be **0"** and the Bullet position **0.25"**.   **(3 Marks)**

p) The following headings **(Equipment and Material, ManPower/Labour and Summary)** should be bold letters and placed in **Small caps**.   **(2 Marks)**

q) Correct all spelling errors in the document.   **(2 Marks)**

r) Save the changes you have made to the file.   **(1 Mark)**

[Sub-Total - (35 Marks)]

SECTION B

The proposal is to be sent to the persons below accompanied by a cover letter:-

- Mr. Paul Henry, The Director, Public Works Department, 5 Binnie Ave., Westtown, Jamaica.

- Mr. Howard Blake, The Honourable Minister, Ministry of Construction, 23 Osbourne Road, Westtown, Jamaica.

- Mr. Vivian Victor, Permanent Secretary, Ministry of Construction, 23 Osbourne Rd, Westtown, Jamaica.

Each cover letter must have the following layout and information. (See page 145.)

Notice that the areas for fields have been identified.

a) Using this letter, create a main document (in preparation for mail merge).
   Name the file PROPOSAL LETTER.   (6 Marks)

b) Create a **data source file** using the names of the individuals to whom the
   letter must be sent. Name the document **PROPOSAL DATABASE**.   (5 Marks)

c) Merge the two documents to produce the three cover letters. Save the
   merged cover letters in a document called **PROPOSAL COVER**.   (4 Marks)

[Sub-Total - (15 Marks)]

[Total - (50 Marks)]

Willsanie Construction Co. Ltd.

5 Jewel Street, Kingston, Jamaica

November 17, 2000.

<Title> <Firstname> <Lastname>

<Position>

<Organisation>

<Address1>

<Address2>

Dear **<Title> <Firstname> <Lastname>**,

Further to your advertisement in the Jamaica Daily Gleaner dated 1 November, 2000, I do hereby submit our proposal for your perusal.

We do sincerely hope that our proposal satisfies all the conditions laid down in your Technical Report. We look forward to attending the meeting dated 20 January, 2001, for the reading of the bids.

Sincerely,

WILLSANIE CONSTRUCTION LTD.

_____

Hector Fitzgerald

CHAPTER 10

TEMPLATES AND WIZARDS

At the end of this chapter you will be able to:-

- Create templates.

- Use Wizards.

TEMPLATES

There are certain types of documents for which a particular layout is consistently utilized, such as letter heads and invoices. Microsoft Word allows you to create and save such a particular layout, once, as a ***template*** and as such it can be reused repeatedly. A template determines the basic structure of a document.

For example, let us imagine that a company's letterhead has been saved as a template with the name ***letterhead***. This means that whenever a company letter has to be typed, the file letterhead can be opened and the letter typed within this document. This is very convenient, as the letterhead does not have to be designed **each time** a company letter is to be typed.

You can create your own template or you can use any of the variety of document templates provided by Microsoft Word.

To use a Template simply:-

1. Select the *File* menu.

2. Click on the *New* command (the *New* dialogue box appears).

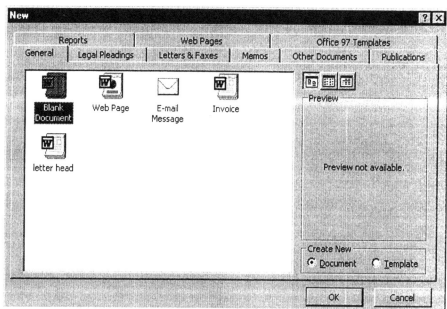

3. The documents are classified under the headings noted on the tabs towards the top of the dialogue box (e.g. **Reports**, and **Letters & Faxes**).

    As you click on each tab button, you would notice several icons representing different types of documents.

To open a document as a template:-

4. Click on its icon.

5. Click on the **Template** option under **Create New**.

6. Click **OK**.

To create your own template:-

1. Create the document that you want to save as a template.

2. Click on the **_File_** menu and **Save _As_**.

3. Type the name of your document.

4. Click on the down arrow in the **Save As type** list box and select **Document Template**.

5. Click on **OK**.

To open a document which you have saved as a template:-

1. Click on the **_File_** menu.

2. Select **_New_**.

3. Under the **General** tab, an icon representing the template you created should be displayed.

4. Click on it and select **OK**.

WIZARDS

Microsoft Word comes with a set of wizards. Wizards are supposed to make it easier for us to create certain documents. Upon starting a wizard you are guided through a series of steps in which you are required to enter data and select from a variety of options. Wizards basically conclude by producing the general layout of a document, including basic information such as the name and address of the sender and recipient (if you were using the Letter Wizard). You would still be required to enter the main content of the document, but at least your work would have been minimized to some degree.

To view the various wizards available:-

1. Click on the **_File_** menu.

2. Select **_New_**. (A dialogue box appears).

3. Click on the various tabs to see the available wizards. For example, click on the **Letters & Faxes** tab. In this area, you should see the **Fax Wizard** and the **Letter Wizard**.

4. To start a particular wizard, click on its icon and then select **OK**.

Before the students can embark upon the revision exercises teachers are asked to type the documents below and save them. Then, copy them to the students' diskettes before each examination practice exercise.

DOCUMENT 1

Step One — Understand Exercise

The **New England** journal of medicine on December 2, 1993, has three articles and five letters showing that jogging, running, heavily pushing cars out of snow, or competitive high-intensive exercise, with shortness of breath from panting, do two bad things to your blood. One, the **platelets** get too sticky, like before a blood clot. Two, there is deficient **plasmin** or clot dissolving enzyme in the blood. What results, there is twice the risk of getting a heart attack within one hour of such immoderate exercise (if you are fit) and more than 120 times the risk if you are a "weekend" exerciser.

Exercise physiology is rediscovering walk. Nothing can take the place of walk. It is a fact that walk helps the heart without endangering it with sticky platelets and compromised plasmin levels.

Step Three — Do it

Action is a law of our being. Living in harmony with this law of physiology will gradually revitalize your whole life. You will feel happier and think better than you have in years. Vitality has a lot to do with success. So, put your action clothes on, slip into those comfortable shoes, and step out into a new life. You will find it more fulfilling, happier, healthier, and more successful than ever.

Step Two — How To Do It

If you are younger than 35, start at once. If you are older just get your family physician's counsel if you have serious heart, lung or joint problems, diabetes or other chronic illness.

Next, understand thoroughly that you are commencing a new life. Steady does it. By walk a little bit today, then a little more tomorrow, and still more the next day you are not going to feel better, you ARE BETTER, from head to toes! The gradual approach to fitness is great for knees, hips, and joints. A variety of exercise forms is even better. Swimming is not only fun, it is splendid exercise. So is cycling and gardening.

INSTRUCTION: Save the document as **HEALTH**.

DOCUMENT 2

Sub-head Introduction

The department of Computer Science at Wildview University carries on a long tradition in the study of computer science. The department is committed to achieving a high level of academic excellence in both research and graduate education. The faculty is actively involved in a number of on-going research projects. Our <u>Master's and Doctoral programmes</u> are designed to provide graduate students with an appropriate level of breadth while at the same time maintaining depth of knowledge in the students' chosen area of specialization.

The department offers programmmes for both the <u>M.A. and Ph.D. degrees</u>. There are approximately 90 graduate students in the department. The department has students from all parts of the world.

Sub-head Financial Information

Tuition and other fees per year for this academic year is $20,000 for the Master's programme and $25,000 for the Ph.D. programme. Graduate Students are required to pay an additional annual charge of $367 for health insurance. Three terms of residence are required for the <u>M.A. programme</u> and six terms of residence for the <u>Ph.D. programme</u>.

Sub-head Computing Facilities

Many computing services and resources are available to graduate students. There is the Social Science Computing Lab, which consists of forty-three terminals which are connected to a powerful mainframe computer. The Lab also contains twenty IBM compatible networked personal computers, which offer word processing and spreadsheet capabilities linked to a HP Deskjet printer.

INSTRUCTION: Save the document as **GRADUATE**.

REVISION EXERCISE 1

SECTION A

Dell View School Health Club is about to distribute the first issue of its newly created quarterly newsletter. The newsletter will cover various health related issues relevant to the student population. The club has put together a basic outline (saved on your diskette as **Health**) of the article to be used in the first issue of the newsletter. You are part of a committee that has been asked to take this basic outline and change it into a newsletter:-

1. You are required to:-

a) Create a new Word processing document and enter the title below as it appears:-

   Would You Like to

   Feel Better, Look Better And Be

   Healthier In Just 10 days?

   Here Is How In Just Three Steps

Note, the title should be bolded, in Small caps and the font size should be **14**.

The rest of the document should use a smaller font size. **(3 Marks)**

b) Set the margins at 0.6-inch all around and the page orientation to Landscape. **(2 Marks)**

c) Insert *Dell View High Quarterly Newsletter, Vol.1, No. 4* as a header at the top left-hand corner of the page. It should be in small caps, bolded and italized. **(4 Marks)**

d) Apply the 1.5" line spacing. **(1 Mark)**

e) The newsletter will be formatted in three newspaper style columns.
   Note that the columns should start after the title created in a) above. **(6 Marks)**

f) The article should be fully-justified. **(1 Mark)**

g) Move the contents of the file **Health** below the title in your new word processing document. **(2 Marks)**

h) Remove the bold and underline from the words **New England**, **plasmin** and **platelets**. (2 Marks)

i) Change all occurrences of the **word** walk to **walking**, (2 Marks)

j) **Capitalize** each step or sub-heading (i.e., Understand Exercise, Do It, etc.). (1 Mark)

k) **Delete** the words **Step One, Step Two** and **Step Three** from the sub-headings. (1 Mark)

l) **Move** the heading and its associated passage **How To Do It** and position it above the heading **Do It**. (2 Marks)

m) Insert a footer at the bottom right-hand corner and type:-
   Dr. Bernell Baldwin, PhD (3 Marks)

n) Perform a **spell check** on the document. (2 Marks)

o) Insert an appropriate picture immediately above the sub-heading **Understand Exercise**. (3 Marks)

p) Save the document as **HEALTH 2**.

[Sub Total - (35 marks)]

SECTION B

The committee has decided to send the first issue of the newsletter to parents free of costs with a cover letter encouraging them to support the newsletter with their financial support and in purchasing future copies.

2. *You are required to:-*

a) Prepare the following cover letter to be used as a mail-merge document.
   Save it to a file called **COVER LETTER**. (6 Marks)

Dell View High School Health Club

174 Olympic Street, Kingston, Jamaica

Tel. (876) 932-1639

Date

<Parent's Name>

<Parent's Address>

Dear <Title> <Surname>

As you are aware, our club has embarked on a project to publish a quarterly newsletter on health related issues. The funds from the newsletter will be used to facilitate the development of our new computer laboratory. We, therefore, respectfully request that you contribute to this venture by subscribing to our newsletter. Futhermore, your son or daughter will find the newsletter immensely beneficial as it covers areas that will help students to utilize their brain power. The club has decided to make the first issue available to parents free of cost and as such please find attached a copy of our first issue. If you are impressed and decide to make a contribution to cover our expenses please contact us.

As usual we look forward to your kind cooperation.

Yours Truly,

David Heslop

President

b) Prepare a secondary document from the following information and save it as PARENTS' DATA.

     I.   Mrs. Mavis Blake, 36 Keane Street, Kingston 2, Jamaica.

    II.   Mr. Horace Victor, 127 Pelican Street, Kingston 9, Jamaica.

    III.   Ms. Winsome McNamarrah, 18 Blue Road, Kingston 23, Jamaica.

    IV.   Mr. Henry Doyles, 4 Wickham Avenue, Kingston 12, Jamaica.

(5 Marks)

c) Merge the two documents to produce the letters to be sent to the parents.
Save the letters as SUPPORT.   **(4 Marks)**

[Sub Total - (15 Marks)]

[Total - (50 Marks)]

REVISION EXERCISE 2

SECTION A

1. You are a clerk in the department of Computer Science at Wildview University. The department is sending out congratulatory letters along with an information brochure to the students who have been accepted in the graduate programme. You have been asked to prepare a two-column brochure to be attached to the letter. A basic outline of the material to be used in this brochure is found in the file **GRADUATE**. You are required to create the brochure from the basic outline.

a) Retrieve the file called **GRADUATE** from your diskette   (1 Mark)

b) Set the top, left and right margins at 1.8" and the bottom margin at 2".   (4 Marks)

c) Change the font size of the text to 13.   (1Mark)

d) Some words were underlined in the file GRADUATE for emphasis.
Remove all the underlining from the passage.   (1 Mark)

e) Insert the heading at the top of the page as it appears below:-

   Wildview University 2001/2002

   General Information

   Computer Science Department

   (The heading should use the font size 15 inch, bolded and in Small caps).   (4 Marks)

f) Left-align, embolden, capitalize and underline all sub-headings.
Each sub-heading is prefixed with the word **Sub-head**.   (4 Marks)

g) The brochure will have several sections with a sub-heading indicating
the start of a new section. Each section will begin on a new page.   (3 Marks)

h) Replace all occurrences of the word **department** with **Department**.   (2 Marks)

i) Move the sub-heading **Computing Facilities** and the passage associated
with it and place before the sub-heading **Financial Information**.   (2 Marks)

j) Immediately following the first paragraph of the sub-heading Financial Information add the following table:-

	Master's	Ph.D.
Tuition	$20,000	$25,000
Health Insurance	$585	$585
Student Services	$235	$300
Registration Fee	$130	$200
Computing Fee	$25	$25

(5 Marks)

k) The following header should appear on each page.
   Computer Science Department (2 Marks)

l) Add a footnote asociated with the first sentence below the sub-heading
   Financial Information. The footnote should read:
   "The University reserves the right to make changes without notice in the published scale of fees." (2 Marks)

m) Remove the word **Sub-head** from the start of each sub-heading. (1 Mark)

n) Correct all spelling errors in the document. (2 Marks)

o) Save the new document as **GRADUATE ONE**. (1 Mark)

[Sub Total - (35 Marks)]

SECTION B

2. a) Enter and save the following document in preparation for a mail merge,
      in a file named **ACCEPT LETTER**. (4 Marks)

   b) The letter should be justified. (2 Marks)

   c) Enter names and addresses of five students in a secondary document named
      GRADUATE STUDENTS. (5 marks)

   d) Merge the two documents to produce the cover letters for the brochures and
      save as **COVER LETTERS**. (4 Marks)

[Sub Total - (15 Marks)]

[Total - (50 Marks)]

2. A cover letter is to accompany each brochure sent to students. Each cover letter will take the form below:

Wildview University

Department of Computer Science

Dellwill Bldg.

Wildview University

Date

<Student Name>

<Student Address>

<Student Address 1>

Dear <Title> <Surname>,

Re: Application

We take this opportunity to congratulate you on your acceptance into the graduate programme beginning August 2001.

Please find attached an information brochure that should be read by all students who are new to the Department of Computer Science. The registration period will take place from 20-25 August. If you are unable to register during the registration period, you may still register from 3-6 September, but you will be assessed a late registration fee of $200.

If you have any questions, do not hesitate to contact us.

Sincerely,

Marva Sousi

Secretary